HOLT SCIENCE & TECHNOLOGY

LONG-TERM PROJECTS & RESEARCH IDEAS

HOLT, RINEHART AND WINSTON

A Harcourt Education Company

Orlando • **Austin** • New York • San Diego • Toronto • London

To the Teacher

The worksheets in this booklet are designed to help students identify topics and conduct research for science projects and papers. This booklet contains a worksheet with ideas for research and long-term projects for each chapter in the *Holt Science and Technology* Pupil's Edition.

RESEARCH IDEAS

By conducting independent research, students can achieve a deeper, richer understanding of scientific topics. These research ideas also offer students the following opportunities:

- ideas and inspirations for topics of further investigation
- practice using library and Internet resources
- engrossing questions to guide their research
- practice writing technical papers

LONG-TERM PROJECTS

Long-term projects provide students with the opportunity to go beyond library and Internet resources to explore scientific topics. Use the long-term project ideas as:

- suggestions for science fair projects
- field trip suggestions for individuals or the entire class
- science explorations carried out in a fun, nontraditional manner
- creative, hands-on projects for curious students in search of alternate learning methods
- ways for students to use multiple media to report their scientific findings

HOW-TO SECTION FOR STUDENTS

Pages xiv–xvii of this booklet are specially designed to help guide students through the process of doing a project or long-term experiment. Some students may have difficulty getting started or may be uncertain how to proceed. This section provides helpful hints on selecting a topic, researching, experimenting, interviewing, and presenting results. If students require additional preparation, you might want to take advantage of the many skill-building activities in the *Science Skills Worksheets* booklet. Worksheets 16–22, 27, and 30 may be particularly helpful to students attempting a long-term project or conducting independent research.

Art Credits
All art, unless otherwise noted, by Holt, Rinehart and Winston.
Abbreviated as follows: (t) top; (b) bottom; (l) left; (r) right; (c) center; (bkgd) background.

Front Cover (zebra), JH Pete Carmichael/Getty Images; (arch), Steve Niedirf Photography/ Getty Images; (aircraft), Creatas/PictureQuest; (owl), Kim Taylor/Bruce Coleman
Page 1 (tl), Michael Kirchhoff; 3 (bl), David Merrell; 6 (tl), Darius Detwiler; 7 (cl), Rosiland Solomon; 8 (tl), David Merrell; 10 (tl), Rosiland Solomon; 12 (tr), Darius Detwiler; 13 (cl), Tom Galgliano; 14 (tr), Rosiland Solomon; 15 (bl), Michael Kirchhoff; 16 (cl), Laurie O'Keefe; 19 (tl), Darius Detwiler; 20 (tl), Rosiland Solomon; 23 (tr), Rosiland Solomon; 24 (cl), Darius Detwiler; 29 (cl), Laurie O'Keefe; 33 (tr), David Merrell; 33 (bl), Rosiland Solomon; 35 (tr), David Merrell; 38 (cl), Rosiland Solomon; 41 (cl), Rosiland Solomon; 42 (bl), Darius Detwiler; 46 (cl), Michael Kirchhoff; 47 (cl), Michael Kirchhoff; 51 (bl), David Chapman; 52 (tl), Michael Kirchhoff; 53 (tr), Tom Galgliano; 55 (cl), Michael Kirchhoff; 56 (cl), Carlyn Iverson; 58 (cl), David Merrell; 59 (cl), Tom Galgliano; 60 (tl), Darius Detwiler; 61 (cl), Tom Galgliano; 61 (bl), Tom Galgliano; 63 (cl), Tom Galgliano; 64 (bl), Darius Detwiler; 65 (bl), Rosiland Solomon; 67 (cl), David Chapman; 71 (cl), David Chapman; 72 (cl), Tom Galgliano; 73 (cl), Tom Galgliano; 74 (cl), Michael Kirchhoff; 75 (tl), Carlyn Iverson; 76 (tr), Michael Kirchhoff; 77 (cl), Michael Kirchhoff; 78 (tr), Michael Kirchhoff

Printed in the United States of America

ISBN 0-03-035191-X   3 4 5 6   085   09 08 07 06 05

• CONTENTS •

LIFE SCIENCE PROJECTS

CONTENTS, CONTINUED

CONTENTS, CONTINUED

Safety Guidelines and Symbols for Students

Performing scientific investigations in the laboratory is exciting and fun, but it can be dangerous if the proper precautions aren't followed. To make sure that your laboratory experience is both exciting and safe, follow the general guidelines listed below. Also follow your teacher's instructions, and don't take shortcuts! When you have read and have understood all of the information in this section, including the Student Safety Contract, sign your name in the designated space on the contract and return the contract to your teacher.

- **GENERAL** Always get your teacher's permission before attempting any laboratory investigation. Before starting a lab, read the procedures carefully, paying attention to safety information and cautionary statements. If you are unsure about what a safety symbol means, look it up here or ask your teacher. If an accident does occur, inform your teacher immediately.

  Know the location of the nearest fire alarms and any other safety equipment, such as fire blankets and eyewash fountains, and the procedure for using them. Know the fire-evacuation routes established by your school. Never work alone in the laboratory. Walk with care, and keep your work area free from all unnecessary clutter. Extra books, jackets, and materials can interfere with your experiment and your work. Dress appropriately on lab day. Tie back long hair. Certain products, such as hair spray, are flammable and should not be worn while working near an open flame. Remove dangling jewelry. Don't wear opened-toed shoes or sandals in the laboratory.

 EYE SAFETY Wear approved safety goggles when working with or around chemicals, any mechanical device, or any type of flame or heating device. If any substance gets in your eyes, notify your teacher. If a spill gets on your skin or clothing, immediately rinse the area with water and have someone notify your teacher.

 HAND SAFETY Avoid chemical or heat injuries to your hands by wearing protective gloves or oven mitts. Check the materials list in the lab for the type of hand protection you should wear while performing the experiment.

 CLOTHING PROTECTION Wear an apron to protect your clothing from staining, burning, or corrosion.

 SHARP/POINTED OBJECTS Use knives and other sharp instruments with extreme care. Do not cut an object while holding it in your hands. Instead, place it on a suitable work surface for cutting.

 HEAT Wear safety goggles when using a heating device or working near a flame. Wear oven mitts to avoid burns.

ELECTRICITY Be careful with electrical wiring. When using equipment with an electrical cord, do not place the cord where it could cause someone to trip. Do not let cords hang over a table edge in a way that could cause equipment to fall if the cord is accidentally pulled. Do not use equipment with damaged cords. Be sure your hands are dry and that electrical equipment is turned off before plugging it into the outlet. Turn off all equipment when you are finished using it.

 CHEMICALS Wear safety goggles when you are handling potentially dangerous chemicals. Read chemical labels. Wear an apron and latex gloves when working with acids or bases or when directed. If a spill gets on your skin or clothing, rinse it off immediately with water for at least 5 minutes while notifying your teacher. Never touch, taste, or smell a chemical unless your teacher instructs you to do so. Never mix any chemical unless your teacher instructs you to do so.

 ANIMAL SAFETY Handle animals only as directed by your teacher. Always treat animals carefully and with respect. Wash your hands thoroughly after handling any animal.

 PLANT SAFETY Wash your hands thoroughly after handling any part of a plant. Do not eat any part of a plant.

■ **GLASSWARE** Examine all glassware before using it. Be sure that it is clean and is free of chips and cracks. Report damaged glassware to your teacher. Glass containers used for heating should be made of heat-resistant glass.

■ **CLEANUP** Before leaving the lab, clean your work area. Wash glass containers with soap and water. Put away all equipment and supplies. Dispose of all chemicals and other materials as directed by your teacher. Make sure water, gas, burners, and hot plates are turned off. Make sure all electrical equipment is unplugged. Wash hands with soap and water after working in the laboratory. Never take anything from the laboratory without permission from your teacher.

Safety Contract

Carefully read the Student Safety Contract below. Print your name in the first blank, and sign and date the contract. Give the Safety Contract to your teacher.

STUDENT SAFETY CONTRACT

I will:

- [ ] read the lab investigation before coming to class.
- [ ] wear personal protective equipment as directed to protect my eyes, face, hands, and body while conducting class activities.
- [ ] follow all instructions given by the teacher.
- [ ] conduct myself in a responsible manner at all times in a laboratory situation.

I, _____,

have read and agree to abide by the safety regulations as set forth above and any additional printed instructions provided by my teacher or the school district.

I agree to follow all other written and oral instructions given in class.

Date: _____

Signature:

_____

SAFETY APPROVED CONTRACT

The Scientific Method

The steps that scientists use to answer questions and solve problems are often called the scientific method. The scientific method is not a rigid procedure. Scientists may use all of the steps or just some of the steps. They may even repeat some steps. The goal of using a scientific method is to come up with reliable answers and solutions.

Six Steps of a Scientific Method

1. Ask a Question Good questions come from careful **observations**. You make observations by using your senses to gather information. Sometimes you may use instruments, such as microscopes and telescopes, to extend the range of your senses. As you observe the natural world, you will discover that you have many more questions than answers. These questions drive the scientific method.

Questions beginning with *what, why, how,* and *when* are very important in focusing an investigation, and they often lead to a hypothesis. (You will learn what a hypothesis is in the next step.) Here is an example of a question that could lead to further investigation.

Question: How does acid rain affect plant growth?

2. Form a Hypothesis After you come up with a question, you need to turn the question into a hypothesis. A **hypothesis** is a clear statement of what you expect the answer to your question to be. Your hypothesis will represent your best "educated guess" based on your observations and what you already know. A good hypothesis is one that is testable. If observations and information cannot be gathered or if an experiment cannot be designed to test your hypothesis, it is untestable, and the investigation can go no further.

Here is a hypothesis that could be formed from the question, "How does acid rain affect plant growth?"

Hypothesis: Acid rain causes plants to grow more slowly.

Notice that the hypothesis provides some specifics that lead to methods of testing. The hypothesis can also lead to predictions. A **prediction** is what you think will be the outcome of your experiment or data collection. Predictions are usually stated in an "if . . . then" format. For example, if meat is kept at room temperature, then it will spoil faster than meat kept in the refrigerator. More than one prediction can be made for a single hypothesis.

Here is a sample prediction for the acid rain hypothesis.

Prediction: If a plant is watered with only acid rain (which has a pH of 4), then the plant will grow at one-half its normal rate.

3. Test the Hypothesis After you have formed a hypothesis and made a prediction, it is time to test your hypothesis. There are different ways to test a hypothesis. Perhaps the most familiar way is by conducting a controlled experiment. A **controlled experiment** is an experiment that tests only one factor at a time. A controlled experiment has a **control group** and one or more experimental groups. All the factors for the control and **experimental groups** are the same except for one factor, which is called the **variable.** By changing only one factor (the variable), you can see the results of just that one change.

Sometimes, a controlled experiment is not possible due to the nature of the investigation. For example, stars are too far away, dinosaurs have been extinct for millions of years, and the Earth's core is surrounded by thousands of meters of rock. It would be difficult if not impossible to do controlled experiments on such things. Under these and many other circumstances, a hypothesis may be tested by making detailed observations. Taking measurements is one way of making observations.

4. Analyze the Results After you have completed your experiments, made your observations, and collected your data, you must analyze all the information you have gathered. Tables and graphs are often used in this step to organize the data.

5. Draw Conclusions Based on the analysis of your data, you should conclude whether your results support your hypothesis. If your hypothesis is supported, you (or others) might want to repeat the observations or experiments to verify your results. If your hypothesis is not supported by the data, you may have to check your procedure for errors. You may even have to reject your hypothesis and make a new one. If you cannot draw a conclusion from your results, you may have to try the investigation again or carry out further observations or experiments.

6. Communicate Results After any scientific investigation, you should report your results. By doing a written or oral report, you let others know what you have learned. They may want to repeat your investigation to see if they get the same results. Your report may even lead to another question, which in turn may lead to another investigation.

How To Do a Long-Term or Research Project

Whether you're getting ready to embark on a long-term project or preparing to do research, here are some tips to guide you along the way.

General Tips

- **Work on something you like.** You'll be working on this project for a while, so make sure you work on a subject you find interesting. Choose a topic that you want to know more about, or consider tackling a topic or question from your science class that puzzles you. Choosing a topic that's right for you can be difficult. If you're having trouble, be sure to talk to your teacher. Your teacher can offer strategies to help you find a good subject.

- **Start early!** If you start your research early, you'll have more time to find the information you need. If you're experimenting, you'll need plenty of time to thoroughly test your hypothesis. Starting early may give you time to redesign your experiment or change topics, just in case something doesn't work out as you planned. You'll also have more time to put together an informative and attractive presentation or paper.

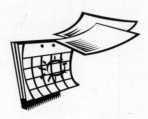

- **Break it down.** For any type of project, it is a good idea to set small goals for yourself instead of conquering the project as a whole. For example, if you have 4 weeks to complete a project, break up the project into four smaller parts. Assign yourself one for each week. Small weekly goals are easier to accomplish than one big project, and they will also help you to monitor your progress.

Research Guidelines

- **Don't believe everything you read.** If a statement sounds fishy to you, question its source. Ask yourself if the source is reliable. Is it a government agency, professional association, museum, or well-known, scientifically accurate magazine? If not, you'll probably need to verify.

- **Keep track of your sources.** A bibliography is a list of sources used in writing a paper. Most teachers require research papers to include a bibliography. Find out what kind of information your teacher expects to see in your bibliography. Before you begin taking notes from a new source, record the source's bibliographical information. A detailed, well-organized bibliography makes your paper more credible. It shows how much work you've put into your research. It also provides a list of resources in case you, your teacher, or another scientist wants to study the topic further.

- **Keep track of your notes.** It is important to know which source your information comes from. One strategy is to keep notes on color-coded note cards. Use colored index cards or design your own system with plain cards and markers. Always keep your notes together so you don't lose them. You may want to use a pocket folder or a three-ring binder to keep your notes in one place.

Internet Research—Finding Reliable Sources

When you do research on the World Wide Web, avoid drawing conclusions before you've checked the information for reliability. Often you can tell when a Web page contains bias or is opinion-based. But in many cases, an author may present his or her ideas as facts while giving little scientific evidence to back them up. When you are uncertain of a source's reliability, consider the following criteria:

Criteria for Reliable Web Pages

- The authors make their case based on adequate evidence.
- The authors interpret the data cautiously.
- The authors acknowledge and deal with opposing views or arguments.
- The authors list current sources that support their claims.

Some characteristics of unreliable Web pages require practice to identify. So put on your thinking cap and question what you read. The following list will clue you in to questionable Web pages:

Characteristics of Unreliable Web Pages

- The authors make extraordinary claims with little supporting evidence.
- The authors relate evidence based on personal experience instead of referencing controlled studies.
- The authors appeal to emotion rather than to logic.
- The authors misrepresent or ignore opposing views.
- The authors' arguments support a politically or financially rewarding viewpoint.

Deciding whether you can rely on information from a Web page may be difficult. But with practice, you'll become very good at spotting unreliable Web pages.

Experimenting Guidelines

- Brainstorm ideas for topics, and write down those ideas in your ScienceLog or in a special lab journal.

- Keep all of your project notes in one place. This will make it easier for you to review the information later as you write a paper, make a presentation, or answer questions.

- Follow the steps of the scientific method.

- Take careful notes during your preliminary research and record your questions and your hypotheses. Keep all of your experimental designs and data in your journal.

- Don't do anything dangerous or unethical. Be sure to obey the safety and experimental guidelines established by your teacher.

- Remember, even if your experiment doesn't support your hypothesis, you will have learned something. Investigate why your hypothesis might have been wrong, and then explain your conclusions in your presentation.

Interviewing Guidelines

- Schedule interviews well in advance. Explain to the person you are interviewing who you are and why you want an interview. Before your interview, do some background research on the person you are interviewing.

- Go to the interview with a prepared list of questions, a notebook, and a pen to jot down your answers. If you want to make a video or audio recording of the interview, be sure to get permission from the person ahead of time.

- During the interview, remember that your prepared list of questions is just to help get you started. Be respectful, and don't be afraid to ask new or follow-up questions.

Presenting Your Results

At this stage, you will turn all your hard work into a product that you will use to share your research with others. Your worksheets offer one or more suggestions for how to present your research. Whether you decide to write a paper or an article, make an oral presentation, or present your results in a series of graphs and tables, be sure to follow the guidelines set by your teacher. Remember to get your teacher's permission before proceeding!

- **What medium should I use?** There are always a variety of options for sharing what you've learned, and you'll want to choose the best medium for highlighting your research. There are many issues to consider when choosing how to present your research. For example, if you are thinking about an audiovisual approach, do you have access to the appropriate equipment? Can you operate the equipment well enough to create a polished presentation? If you want to reflect your findings in the form of a play, story, or other creative work, will that medium allow you to adequately share what you learned? Or would a traditional method of presenting scientific research—such as a paper, poster, or oral presentation—be more suitable? Think carefully about which medium would be most appropriate for the research you have done.

- **What about length requirements?** Do enough research to allow you to explain the topic thoroughly. If your paper should be four pages long, rewrite and revise your paper until it is four pages long. If your oral presentation should take 10 minutes, practice your oral presentation and make sure that it is 10 minutes long. If you find that you don't have enough information to meet the length requirements of your project, you may have to do more research. A good way to avoid this problem is by starting with more research than you think you will need. Then cut out the extra or less important information.

- **How do I present my work scientifically?** Remember that scientific writing is different than creative writing. Be sure to state the facts, and be clear about what information is factual and what is your opinion. Show how the evidence you gathered supports your conclusions. If you are using graphs or tables, make sure they are easy to read. Give details about how and where you got your information. Even if you are presenting your findings in a creative manner, you must still document your sources and be able to explain the science behind your work.

Now you are ready to take part in a very important part of science— research. Good luck and have fun!

PROJECT
1 **STUDENT WORKSHEET**

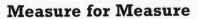

DESIGN YOUR OWN

The Length of a Fethel

Paris, France, July 26, 2033. After three weeks, the world is still amazed at the discovery of a hidden civilization of intelligent creatures living underground on an island off the coast of France. Called Singelapins by locals, they have thrived for millennia untouched by above-ground society. Their name means "ape-bunnies," which is fitting since they look like gorillas but have long, rabbitlike ears on the top of their heads. Anthropologists and ambassadors have been trying to communicate with this strange subterranean society. They have learned a little about the Singelapinian measuring systems. For example, the basic Singelapinian unit of length is the *fethel,* which is the average length of one of a Singelapin's ears.

Measure for Measure

1. Sharing scientific discoveries in the ancient world would probably have been a lot harder than it is now. The ancient Egyptians, Babylonians, Greeks, and Chinese had their own measuring systems. How did those ancient measuring systems develop? What other systems came into common use over the centuries? What caused systems to become standardized? How did standardization lead to the development of the International System of Units, or SI? How do past systems compare with SI? Share what you've learned in the form of a poster display.

Long-Term Project Ideas

2. What if our system of measurement was based on the volume of a goldfish, the mass of a kernel of corn, and the length of a videocassette? Develop your own system of measurement for mass, length, and volume. Name your system, and then design an all-in-one device that measures the mass, volume, and length of an object using your system. Your device cannot use any standard measurement tools such as a ruler or measuring cup as part of the design. You should be able to measure the volume of a cube and an irregularly shaped object. Write a manual to explain how to use your machine. Be sure to include a brief explanation of the "origin" of your measuring system as well as a table for converting units in your system to SI units.

The Length of a Fethel, continued

INTERNET KEYWORDS

Frogwatch USA

NARCAM

NAAMP

National Wildlife Federation

3. Many amphibian species are disappearing, and frogs with deformities are being found at an increased rate. Help scientists solve the puzzle of the oddly-shaped and disappearing amphibians! Get involved with one of the following amphibian monitoring programs: Frogwatch USA, North American Reporting Center for Amphibian Malformations (NARCAM), or the North American Amphibian Monitoring Program (NAAMP). Use the Internet to find out more information about each program and the guidelines for participation. If you're not a frog fan, check into the National Wildlife Federation's list of other monitoring programs. Make a poster outlining theories on the cause or causes of the decline in amphibian populations.

4. Who are life scientists, and what do they do? Use library and Internet resources to research the life and work of one of the life scientists listed below or another life scientist who interests you. Familiarize yourself with the country and culture in which the scientist lived, major events in the scientist's life, and the ideas that the scientist studied and developed. Then with a partner, write a script for an imaginary interview with the scientist. Include simple and safe demonstrations of the important scientific ideas. Dress in costume and videotape the interview or perform it live for your classmates.

Name	Field
Elizabeth Blackwell	Medicine
Cornelia Clapp	Zoology
Charles Darwin	Biology
Alexander Fleming	Bacteriology
Jane Goodall	Anthropology
Mae C. Jemison	Aeronautics and medicine
Ernest Everett Just	Biology
Barbara McClintock	Genetics
Thomas Hunt Morgan	Zoology and genetics
Mary Walker	Medicine
James D. Watson	Genetics

Name _____ Date _____ Class _____

DESIGN
YOUR OWN

I Think, Therefore I Live

In May 1997, an IBM supercomputer called Deep Blue defeated the world chess champion, Gary Kasparov, in a highly publicized chess match. Game playing is one branch of the high-tech field of computing called artificial intelligence, or AI. AI is concerned with programming computers to think and behave like humans. Computers with artificial intelligence are helping doctors with diagnoses. In robotics, artificial intelligence is being used to program robots to see, hear, and react to sensory stimuli. And incredibly, computer systems are being designed to simulate intelligence based on the reproduction of the types of physical connections that occur in animals' brains.

LIFE SCIENCE

INTERNET KEYWORDS
artificial intelligence
cybernetics
neural networks

Living Computers?

1. Can computers really think like people? Will future thinking machines force us to redefine living? Use Internet and library resources to research the subject of artificial intelligence. What can the human brain do that a computer can't do? What is the future of artificial intelligence? Write a report presenting your findings.

Other Research Ideas

2. Do you think you have too much fat in your diet? Many health experts warn that eating too much saturated fat can be hazardous to your health. Use library and Internet resources to research the average diets of people from the United States, Japan, and the Mediterranean region (Greece, Italy, France, Portugal, and Spain). How are the types of food—meats, vegetables, fruits, etc.—different in each diet? What differences are there in the amounts of fats, carbohydrates, and proteins consumed? What effects do these differences have on health? Write a news article explaining your findings.

3. Feeling the heat? Your body sweats to cool down. Feeling a chill? Your body shivers to warm up. In hot or cold conditions, your body tries to maintain its normal temperature. But what happens when it can't? What are heat exhaustion, heat stroke, chilblains, and frostbite? How are these conditions treated, and how can you protect yourself from getting them in the first place? Find out the answers to these questions and then demonstrate to the class how to avoid hazards and "play it safe" in extreme temperatures. The American Red Cross might be a good source of information. Videotape your presentation, if possible.

I Think, Therefore I Live, continued

Long-Term Project

4. Are eggs the breakfast of champions? Does orange juice kick-start your day? Design a 4- to 6-week experiment to investigate the effects of different breakfasts on your energy level in the morning. You might want to conduct this experiment with a group of classmates to get a larger data sample.

a. Plan what breakfast you will test each week. For example, the first week's breakfast might be one bowl of cereal with milk and two pieces of toast with butter. The second week, it might be two scrambled eggs with one glass of orange juice. It's important that you eat the same breakfast for 7 days in a row. Varying the meal within a particular week will weaken the validity of your results.

b. Develop a list of 5 to 10 questions that you will answer each hour to evaluate your energy level. For example, how alert are you? How well are you able to concentrate or focus? How well can you remember things? Do you feel tired? Write those questions in a notebook that you will use to keep a record of your data.

c. During the experiment, spend a few minutes every hour before lunch recording your responses to your list of questions from Step b. Rate your response to each question on a scale of 1 to 5, 1 being the least and 5 being the most. Also, note anything that might influence your data. A sample entry is shown below. Don't forget to record data right before and after you eat! Also remember that there are no right or wrong answers. When collecting scientific data, record what actually happens.

Sample Breakfast Data Chart

Date	Time	Ratings	Notes
March 3, 2000	10 A.M.	Alertness 4 Memory 4 Ability to concentrate 5	I'm having an easy time understanding everything today, but it could be because it's my favorite class (math).

d. After you finish the experiment, evaluate your data. Which breakfast gave you the most energy? Is this what you expected? Which particular food do you think affected your energy level the most? Present your findings to the class. Be sure to include visual aids, such as graphs, in your presentation.

Name _____ Date _____ Class _____

Ewe Again, Dolly?

In 1997, the Scottish scientist Ian Wilmut announced that he had cloned a sheep named Dolly. Cloning is based on the procedure of *nuclear transfer*. The nucleus of an egg cell is replaced with a nucleus from another cell.

To clone Dolly, Wilmut took an immature, unfertilized egg cell from a 6-year-old ewe and removed the DNA. Next, he took a cell from the ewe's udder and combined the udder cell with the egg cell. The combined cell formed an embryo, which was transplanted into a surrogate ewe. Five months later, Dolly was born—and history was made.

USEFUL TERMS
ewe   female sheep   **surrogate**   an unrelated animal that acts as a parent

LIFE SCIENCE

INTERNET KEYWORDS
cloning   cloning and ethics   human cloning   organ cloning

To Clone or Not to Clone?

1. What if a scientist could take a few human cells and make an exact copy of you or anyone else? What concerns do people have about human cloning? Research the controversy surrounding human cloning, and then prepare a display that presents arguments for and against human cloning. Be sure to support each argument with evidence.

Other Research Ideas

2. How do cells in an embryo know where to go? Why don't you find brain cells in your stomach or stomach cells in your brain? A German scientist named Guenter Albrecht-Buehler looked for the answers to these questions. Find out about Albrecht-Buehler's discovery. Write a report about his hypothesis, his experiment, and other scientist's opinions about his work.

3. Sometimes the only way to save a patient with a poorly working organ is to transplant another person's healthy organ. But a transplanted organ isn't always accepted by the patient's body. Research the latest advances in organ transplantation. Why is the procedure so difficult? Which organs have the highest acceptance and rejection rates? What technologies are producing a higher survival rate for patients? Write a news article about your research.

Long-Term Project Idea

4. Have you ever pulled out food from the freezer only to discover that the food was ruined because of freezer burn? What causes freezer burn? How does freezing affect the cells of different kinds of food? Design an experiment to test how quickly different foods, such as vegetables or meat, are damaged by freezer burn. How does the type of wrapping affect the speed of freezer burn? Write your results in the form of a scientific journal article.

Name _____ Date _____ Class _____

Taming the Wild Yeast

If you have ever made bread, you probably used a packet of dried yeast that you bought at the grocery store. When you add warm water and sugar to the dried yeast, the yeast begin the process of fermentation. And as you know, the products of fermentation, carbon dioxide and alcohol, give the bread its texture and flavor. But bread has been around a lot longer than those yeast packets. How do you think people made leavened bread before they could buy yeast at the store? Would you believe they actually captured their own yeast from the wild? In fact, bread bakers would always keep a batch of live yeast around. They would use a bit of their "pet yeast" each time they made bread and then keep the rest for their next loaf. Some yeast cultures have been in families for generations!

Pet Yeast

1. Try your hand at raising yeast. Find a recipe for a sourdough starter in a bread cook book and follow its instructions for culturing wild yeast. If you have trouble culturing wild yeast, you can use dry yeast for your starter. Observe the starter for a few days and record any changes in appearance or odor. Divide the starter into two parts. Add sugar to one and feed the other normally. Is there any difference in the way the yeast react to the two diets? Summarize your findings in a report and share them with the class. Finally, use your pet yeast to make bread, following your favorite recipe.

Another Long-Term Project Idea

2. How do you think different cells of different organisms look during mitosis? As you know, different organisms have different numbers of chromosomes. They also can have slightly different cell structures. Choose one organism and design a creative demonstration of mitosis and the cell cycle for that organism. Perform the demonstration for the class. Be sure to include an explanation of what is happening to each cell structure during each step in mitosis.

Research Idea

3. How can you make salt water drinkable? One way is through reverse osmosis. But what does it take to make osmosis go backwards? What is a semipermeable membrane, and how is it involved? Find out more about how reverse osmosis is used in water purification. Then write a brochure that explains reverse osmosis and how it compares to the osmosis that occurs in your cells.

PROJECT
5 **STUDENT WORKSHEET**

Portrait of a Dog

Take a look at a photograph of an English bulldog. English bulldogs are short and stocky, and they have a tremendous underbite. Now look at a photograph of a greyhound. Greyhounds are tall, slender, and sleek—dogs built for speed! Although the bulldog and the greyhound are different breeds, they are members of the same species. For thousands of years humans have selectively bred dogs for certain traits and with specific tasks in mind. In fact, humans have developed more than 100 different dog breeds!

A Dog's World

1. Did you know that dachshunds were originally bred to follow foxes into foxholes? Use Internet and library resources to research a particular dog breed. What are the breed's unique characteristics? What job was the breed intended to perform? How do the breed's characteristics make it well suited for its job? Does the breed tend to have any problems? If so, why might the breed have these problems, and how can they be corrected? Write a report explaining your findings, and include illustrations of the breed you researched.

Another Research Idea

2. How would you feel if your genes had to pass a test for you to get medical coverage? Use Internet and library resources to research the controversy surrounding genetic testing. Should the results of genetic tests be made available to insurance companies? What information do insurance companies currently use when deciding to insure a person? Should an insurance company be able to refuse or cancel insurance based on the results of a genetic test? Pick one side of this controversy, and be prepared to defend your opinion in a class debate.

INTERNET KEYWORDS
genetic testing
genetic testing insurance
genetic testing medical coverage

A Long-Term Project Idea

3. Some couples have serious health problems in their family history. These couples can meet with a *genetic counselor* to find out the risk of passing on the problems to their children. What kind of background is needed to be a genetic counselor? How does a genetic counselor put together and present information to prospective parents? What is the most difficult part of the job? Interview a genetic counselor, and then write a job description that explains his or her professional roles and responsibilities.

Name _____ Date _____ Class _____

The Antifreeze Protein

The arctic cod and the antarctic notothenioid produce a protein that prevents them from freezing in cold ocean waters. Although these fishes are not closely related and live on opposite sides of the planet, they produce the same "antifreeze" protein. Scientists think the antifreeze protein evolved from a digestive enzyme called trypsinogen.

Nonfrozen Fish

1. Use Internet and library resources to find out more about the antifreeze protein. How does this protein keep the arctic cod and the antarctic notothenioid from freezing? Do any other animals have similar adaptations? Write a magazine article about your findings.

INTERNET KEYWORD
tumor
p53

Other Research Ideas

2. Can you get tumors because of your genes? Investigate the connection between the gene for protein 53 (p53), and the development of tumors. How does the p53 gene work? Why is it so important? What have scientists discovered about the molecules that interact with p53? Are there any drugs being developed in connection with p53? Create a poster display to share your findings with the class.

3. Gene technology can be a powerful tool in medicine. In gene therapy, scientists use properly functioning genetic material to try to repair faulty material in a person's genes. Investigate which diseases are currently being targeted for gene therapy. What are the challenges to gene therapy? How successful is gene therapy? Write an article about gene therapy for your school newspaper.

Long-Term Project Idea

4. Should food be genetically engineered? Should people? Research a genetic-engineering issue that is being debated in the news, such as eugenics or genetically engineered food. Make sure that you understand both sides of the debate. Conduct a survey about the issue in your neighborhood or over the Internet. Analyze the results of your survey. Do people in different age groups tend to have different opinions about this topic? If you conduct the survey over the Internet, consider publishing your results and a copy of the survey on your school's Web page. Using knowledge of the issue and the results of your survey, write a position paper about the issue. Submit your paper to the school newspaper for publication.

PROJECT 7 — STUDENT WORKSHEET

DESIGN YOUR OWN

Evolution's Explosion

Evolution can be a long, gradual process. However, rates of evolution vary, and sometimes, evolution progresses explosively! Single-celled organisms first appeared on Earth about 3.5 billion years ago and dominated the planet for the next 3 billion years. Suddenly, at the beginning of the Cambrian period about 540 million years ago, life began to take new, multicellular shapes. The fossil record shows that over a period of only 5 million to 10 million years, representatives of all the modern animal groups appeared. This giant leap in diversification happened in such a short period of geologic time that it is known as the Cambrian explosion.

LIFE SCIENCE ▲▲▲▲

INTERNET KEYWORDS
Cambrian explosion
punctuated equilibrium
gradualism

The Cambrian Explosion

1. Using the Internet and library resources, research the theories about the Cambrian explosion. What are the reasons for such a rapid diversification of life? What were the conditions on the Earth at the time of the Cambrian explosion? Write a news article about your findings.

Other Research Ideas

2. A species of salamander in California, *Ensatina escholtzi,* appears to be evolving into a number of different species. How do biologists define *species*? Is there more than one definition? Have the salamanders developed into different species?

3. Charles Darwin learned a lot from the Galápagos Islands in the nineteenth century. Research the Galápagos Islands. What kinds of plants and animals live there today? Is anyone studying them now? How have the species on the Galápagos Islands changed since the publication of *On the Origin of Species*? Imagine you have just visited the Galápagos Islands. Write a letter to Darwin explaining how things have changed since he was last there. Be sure to discuss the factors that have led to these changes.

Long-Term Project Idea

4. What were early humans like? What were we like before we could even be called humans? Visit a museum of natural history and study fossils of early humans. Or, interview a paleontologist about the future of human evolution. What factors determined how humans evolve? Are there different theories of human evolution? What is the evidence for those theories? Present your findings as a science magazine article or a videotaped documentary.

Name _____ Date _____ Class _____

A Horse Is a Horse

Horses haven't always had hooves. In the tropical forests of the Eocene epoch, a many-toed creature about the size of a dog fed on soft tree leaves. Scientists call it *Hyracotherium,* but we also know it as *Eohippus,* the dawn horse. *Hyracotherium* was an ancient ancestor of the modern horse.

USEFUL TERM

paleontologist
a scientist who studies the fossil record

An Ancient Ancestor

1. All animals living today are descendants of ancient animals. Some of these animals looked different from their modern descendants. Pick a modern mammal, and trace its evolution. Illustrate its evolution using a family tree. How does the modern animal differ from its ancient ancestor? What other animals have evolved from the same common ancestor? Create a poster of your findings.

Other Research Ideas

2. Have you ever found a fossil of a plant or animal? Are you interested in the Earth's ancient past? Maybe you would enjoy being a paleontologist! Research the career of a paleontologist, such as Charles Walcott, O. C. Marsh, or E. D. Cope. Write a paper about the paleontologist's life and contributions to the field.

3. Should we do everything possible to protect a species from extinction? Will extinction occur no matter what humans do? Research this debate. Form an opinion and write a position paper defending your opinion. Be sure to include examples of controversial efforts to protect endangered species such as the spotted owl.

4. Did a comet kill the dinosaurs? In 1980, Luis Alvarez hypothesized that every 26 million years an unknown celestial object passes near our solar system, bringing along a host of comets. According to this theory, whenever this object approaches, comets bombard the Earth. The result is mass destruction and extinction of many species. Research the evidence Alvarez used to develop this theory. Write a magazine article about your findings.

Long-Term Project Idea

5. Which part of the history of life on Earth do you find most interesting? Visit a local museum or an on-line natural history museum. Take a look at the exhibits about the history of the Earth. Create either a video documentary or a series of short articles about your favorite exhibits. In your presentation, be sure to explain the scientific information in each exhibit.

PROJECT
9 **STUDENT WORKSHEET**

DESIGN YOUR OWN

The Panda Mystery

Picture a raccoon, scurrying around in the woods, getting into campers' food and trash cans. Now imagine a brown bear—enormous and clumsy. They are pretty different animals, right? Maybe not. In 1869, a biologist named Pere David, who was one of the first Europeans to study the giant panda of China, attempted to classify the giant panda as a bear. Other scientists then pointed out that the animal's bones and teeth more closely resembled those of a raccoon. Since then, no one could agree on which animal the giant panda more closely resembled.

Confusing the matter further is the red panda, which behaves much like the giant panda but has even more raccoonlike features. These relationships have led many scientists to group the red panda and giant panda together as relatives of the raccoon. But this isn't the end of the story. So, is the giant panda a bear or a raccoon? What about the red panda?

LIFE SCIENCE ▲ ▲ ▲

INTERNET KEYWORDS
DNA hybridization
panda evolution

Solve the Mystery

1. In the 1980s, a group of scientists used molecular methods of classification, including DNA hybridization and immunological comparisons, to examine the relationships between the giant panda and the red panda. How do these methods of classification work? What did they help scientists discover about the evolution of the giant panda and the red panda? What other applications do these methods have? Write a news article to share your findings with your class.

Other Research Ideas

INTERNET KEYWORDS
muntjac
saola
classification

2. Believe it or not, three new large mammals were recently discovered in Vietnam. The *muntjac,* a barking deer, the *giant muntjac,* its larger relative, and the *saola,* a goatlike creature, are among 10 large mammals that have been discovered in the twentieth century. Learn more about these newly discovered mammals, and research the process that was used to classify them. How often are new species discovered? How many new species are estimated to be out there? Present your research in the form of a nature video, magazine article, or oral presentation.

Long-Term Project

3. You probably don't realize how many forms of life inhabit your own neighborhood! Use a field guide or classification manual to identify 10 animal species found in your neighborhood. Then make a field guide that includes where to find the 10 species in your neighborhood, as well as information such as scientific names and interesting facts. Be creative!

PROJECT
10 **STUDENT WORKSHEET**

Bacteria to the Rescue!

Imagine the aftermath of a supertanker accident. The clear blue ocean turns a murky black. The sea blazes with flames. Millions of liters of spilled oil threaten the lives of fish, birds, and other sea life. But microscopic organisms—bacteria—may be able to save them. Believe it or not, some bacteria eat oil like it was ice cream. Genera like *Pseudomonas* and *Penicillium* love oil spills and can actually make them disappear. Using bacteria to clean up pollution is called *bioremediation*.

INTERNET KEYWORDS
bioremediation
oil spill cleanup
ocean pollution

An Oily Feast

1. How does bioremediation work? In what situations does bioremediation work best? On which major oil spills has it been used? Is it more or less effective than more traditional cleanup methods? Are there disadvantages to using bioremediation? Ask your teacher to obtain cultures of bacteria that are used to clean up oil spills, or to get an oil spill kit from a scientific supply house. Create a model oil spill and use the bacteria to clean the oil from the water. Summarize the effectiveness of this form of bioremediation in a paper, stating your criteria and supporting your claims.

Other Long-Term Project Ideas

2. Are you being exposed to more germs than you should be? Visit a restaurant and either a hospital or biology lab, and compare the procedures used for sanitation at each. Ask a staff member to demonstrate the steps taken to prevent the spread of bacteria and viruses. How are the sanitation standards different? Do you think that each institution's procedures are thorough enough? Prepare a display board that shows what you have learned.

3. Your drinking water may have been through bioremediation! Visit a water treatment plant that uses bioremediation in its processing. Interview the water treatment manager. Tour the plant, taking pictures or videotaping during your tour, and prepare a presentation or documentary to share your discoveries with the class.

Research Idea

4. The bacterial and viral diseases that Europeans brought to the Americas devastated Native American populations. Native Americans had never been exposed to these diseases, and therefore, they had no resistance to them. Write a historical account of the devastation of an American Indian community as a result of contact with foreign diseases.

PROJECT

11 **STUDENT WORKSHEET**

DESIGN YOUR OWN

LIFE SCIENCE ▲▲▲▲

Algae for All!

What do pond scum, red tide, and the green stuff growing in your aquarium have in common? They all are types of algae! As a matter of fact, algae are valuable members of the biosphere. Unfortunately, algae don't always receive the recognition they deserve. Did you know that half the world's organic material produced by photosynthesis comes from algae? And humans use algae more than you might think. We use algae to make medicines as well as to treat sewage. Many cultures eat seaweed and other algae regularly. And though they thrive in watery places like lakes and ponds, these hardy creatures can live almost anywhere—from the Antarctic to the Sahara Desert!

USEFUL TERMS

dermatologist
a doctor who specializes in the skin and its diseases

pathologist
a doctor who specializes in the effects of diseases on the body

Algae Blooms

1. How do algae and detergent mix? Design an experiment to determine the effects of detergent in waste water on algae and other pond plants, such as *Elodea*. Repeat your experiment to test for the effects of fertilizers or acid rain. Present your findings in a scientific article.

More Long-Term Projects

2. Athlete's foot is an itchy infection caused by a fungus. Interview a dermatologist or pathologist about other human diseases that are caused by fungi or by protozoa. Create a brochure for patients with a fungal- or protozoan-related disease that explains the disease and its treatment.

3. You may not realize it, but you probably eat algae on a regular basis. No kidding! Carrageenan, mannitol, and agar are a few algae extracts commonly used in food products. Look for these extracts and other algae-related products on the labels of food and cosmetic containers. Identify and list products in your home that contain algae. Create a poster that highlights at least five of the products in your home that use or contain algae.

Research Idea

4. Sometimes an organ-transplant patient suffers from organ rejection, even though a new organ can save the patient's life! Why does the body do this? How can the drug cyclosporine, derived from a fungus, help the transplant operation to be more successful? Find out about cyclosporine, and research other medical uses of fungi. Write a newspaper article about your findings.

*DESIGN
YOUR OWN*

Plant Planet

Did you know that you can eat dandelions? It's true—fresh dandelion leaves make a tasty salad, and the roots can be boiled to make tea. In fact, many of the plants we think of as weeds can be used in dyes, foods, or medicines.

To Dye For

1. Do some research on making plant-based dyes. Prepare five plant-based dyes from plants you collected or purchased from a grocer or greenhouse. Make a display with a picture of each plant and a sample of the dye color it makes.

Another Long-Term Project Idea

2. Visit a woodland, park, field, or pond, and make detailed drawings and descriptions of 10 wild plants. Remember to include the following: size, shape, and coloring of the plant; leaf size and shape; flower, fruit, or nut size; special features of the stem or trunk; and the date and location you found the plant. Use a plant field guide for your area to identify the 10 plants. Look up each plant's scientific name, its common name, how it reproduces, and where and when it grows. Then find out if the plant is edible to animals or humans and if the plant has any other uses (medicinal, dyeing, clothmaking). Make a small field guide about the 10 plants, including your sketches and the results of your research.

Research Ideas

3. Plants were used to treat diseases long before modern medicines were developed. Research the medicinal uses of plants. What products have been developed from rainforest plants or underwater plants? How effective are medicinal plants compared with more traditional medicines? Write a news article highlighting your findings.

4. Where does your food come from? You might get your food at a supermarket, but most foods in supermarkets originally come from farms. Research current methods of growing food in the United States. How big is the average American farm? What is commonly used for pest control and fertilizer in the United States? Are there effective alternative methods available? Design an informative brochure that explains your findings. You may want to compare the agricultural system of the United States with that of another country.

SAFETY ALERT!

Avoid poison oak, poison ivy, and poison sumac. Also avoid allergen-producing plants, such as ragweed, and plants containing thorns.

HELPFUL HINT

If you have trouble finding a plant in the field guide, it may be helpful to find out the plant's common name.

Name _____ Date _____ Class _____

Plant Partners

You enjoy the benefits of grafting when you eat some fruits. In *grafting,* the stem of one plant and the root of another are united and grow as one plant. Fruit growers take the stem from a tree with desirable fruit and insert it into the rooted stem of another plant. When fitted together, both plants' transport systems allow nutrients to move between them. The grafted stem then grows branches that are identical to the donor fruit tree. Grafting is a form of cloning plants, but it's not a new technique. In fact, grafting has been used by some cultures for thousands of years!

▲ **LIFE SCIENCE**
▲
▲

HELPFUL HINT

You may also try grafting any other plant from the genus *Ipomea.*

SAFETY ALERT!

Use caution when working with sharp knives.

Sweet Potato Glory

1. See if you can graft buds from a sweet potato *(Ipomea batatas)* plant to a morning glory *(Ipomea fistulosa)* bush. Use a sharp knife to remove two buds from the sweet potato. Prepare the morning glory plant by cutting two stems beneath the buds. Graft the sweet potato buds onto the morning glory stems by connecting them with masking tape. Observe the grafted buds carefully over a period of 2 months. Did the graft work? Report your results in the form of a science article.

Another Long-Term Project Idea

2. Can you identify the parts of a flower? Buy a lily from a flower shop or grocery store. Dissect it so that you can see each individual part. Draw the flower, and indicate the anthers, stigma, style, ovary, petals, and sepals in your drawing. Perform a similar dissection on a wildflower. How do its parts compare in color, size, and shape with the lily's? Present your findings as an entry in a field guide on flowers. Be sure to include your illustrations.

Research Ideas

3. Plants in space?! Do they have a spacesuit that would fit? Find out about the experiments astronauts have done on growing plants in low gravity. What problems did they find? Why are astronauts interested in solving these problems? What controls plant responses to gravity? Present your findings in the form of a news article.

4. Some plants can be so touchy. You know plants respond to gravity and light, but how do some respond to touch? What kinds of plants respond to touch? How does wind affect plant growth? Research thigmotropism. How do some plants use it to survive? Prepare a poster display of your findings. Be sure to include illustrations of the different kinds of plant responses to touch.

USEFUL TERMS

thigmotropism
directional growth of a plant in response to touch

Name _____ Date _____ Class _____

Animal-Myth Behaviors

Have you heard about lemmings—small mammals that live in the Arctic and that gather by the thousands every few years to make suicide jumps into icy rivers? Do you think it's true? Well, not completely. When a population of lemmings gets too big, many of them migrate to find food, sometimes crossing large streams or lakes in their search. Countless lemmings die in this bold attempt to find food, which led some people to believe that the lemmings were throwing themselves into the water on purpose.

Fact or Fiction?

1. Do vampire bats drink human blood? Can salamanders walk through fire? Do Texas horned toads spit blood from their eyes? You may have heard a lot of amazing stories about animals—but are they true? Investigate some of the fantastic animal behaviors you've heard about and find out the facts. Write an article for your school paper describing the animals' unusual behaviors.

Another Research Idea

2. How have wild animals adapted to urban and suburban environments? Research animals that have suffered a loss of natural habitat, such as squirrels, coyotes, hawks, raccoons, deer, and pigeons. Which animals have adapted well to living among humans and which have not? Why are some animals more successful at city living than others? Create a poster display highlighting your findings.

Long-Term Project Ideas

3. Research shows that contact with a pet has a calming effect on people. Design and carry out an experiment to test how holding an animal affects the heart rate and blood pressure of people. You might want to test the human response to different animals, being sure to keep all of the other factors the same. Share your findings by using charts, graphs, and photos.

> **HELPFUL HINT**
> Focus on specific behaviors, like how it eats, when and how long it sleeps, how often it moves around, and how it responds to people.

4. Do animals act differently in captivity than they do in the wild? Pick an active animal at a zoo, and observe and record its behaviors for an hour. Then research the animal's natural behavior. Do the behaviors in the zoo match the behaviors you'd expect to see in the wild? If not, can you think of reasons for the differences? Videotape your zoo animal, and share the tape with your class. If possible, also show video footage of your animal in the wild. Include a description of the animal's natural and captive behaviors.

PROJECT 15 **STUDENT WORKSHEET**

DESIGN YOUR OWN

LIFE SCIENCE

Creepy, Crawly Food?

How about having ants for lunch? Or maybe you prefer fried grasshoppers for dinner? Although insects may not be your idea of a great meal, they are an important food source in many parts of the world. Insect larvae, locusts, crickets, termites, and grasshoppers are just a few of the many insects that are eaten by humans. Dig in!

Bugs for Dinner?

1. Research several cultures in which insects are part of people's regular diet. Why do they eat insects? How are the insects prepared? What is their nutritional value? Discuss your findings in a report, and include at least two recipes that contain insects as ingredients.

Research Ideas

2. What does a mollusk have to do with photography? For centuries, people have made products from mollusks. Pearls and mother-of-pearl are used in jewelry, and octopuses release a black fluid that was once used to make ink. Discover the connections between mollusks and photography, and then research at least nine other mollusk products. Make a poster display of your findings, and include samples, photos, or illustrations of the products.

3. The Great Barrier Reef, off the coast of Australia, supports an incredible variety of marine life. It takes an incredible number of coral skeletons, and sometimes millions of years, to build a coral reef. Find out how coral reefs are formed and why they are endangered. Present your research in the form of a news article.

4. Most people try to avoid leeches, little wormlike creatures that suck blood. But did you know that leeches were used to treat illnesses in the eighteenth and nineteenth centuries? Use library resources to find out how and why leeches were used and how they are being used today. Write a report about your findings.

5. If a scorpion stung you, would you know what to do? Research how the sting or bite of an arachnid, such as a scorpion or spider, affects the human body. How dangerous are these animals to humans? What do they use their poison for? Find out what you should do if you are bitten, and write a safety brochure outlining your findings.

PROJECT

16 **STUDENT WORKSHEET**

DESIGN
YOUR OWN

Go Fish!

You're wading at the edge of a lake when suddenly you see a silvery streak dart through the water—a fish! And it looks like a big one! Slowly and quietly, you wade closer. Wait a minute! That streak of silver isn't one big fish after all—it's a large group of tiny fish swimming together in a school. Because the small fish turn together, they appear to be a single, larger fish.

Back to School

1. Visit a local aquarium and observe the schooling behavior of different fishes. You will need to observe a large tank that contains at least 10 fish each of two different species. How does a lone fish act toward members of its own species? How does a lone fish react to members of a different species? Research how the fish behave in the wild. Are there differences between their schooling behavior in the wild and their schooling behavior in the aquarium? If so, what do you think would account for those differences? Create a poster display to present your findings.

Research Ideas

2. Wear those fabulous alligator-skin boots, and you could be breaking the law! Many reptiles are protected species, and killing them is illegal. Find out about protected reptile species. How are they hunted illegally, and what is being done to protect them? Present the information in the form of an article for a hunting or environmental magazine.

3. It's an invasion! Lampreys from the Atlantic Ocean have invaded the Great Lakes! "But that's impossible," you say. "The Atlantic isn't even connected to the Great Lakes!" Find out how the lampreys got into the lakes, the problems lampreys are causing, and what scientists are doing to fix the problems. Report your findings to the class in a special news report.

4. Watch out for those fangs! Although only a few of the 3,000 known species of snakes are poisonous, it takes only one snake to endanger a human life. Surviving a venomous snake bite may require an injection of *antivenin,* an antitoxin for snake venom. Many antivenins are manufactured in unusual ways. Investigate how antivenins are made, how they work, and how effective they are. Write a science news article about your findings.

PROJECT 17 — STUDENT WORKSHEET

DESIGN YOUR OWN

LIFE SCIENCE ▲▲▲

Look Who's Coming to Dinner

"Please pass the sunflower seeds." "Stop spitting!" "Would you PLEASE close your beak while you eat?" You can learn a lot about birds by watching them eat together. A good place to observe bird behavior is at a bird feeder. Some animals other than birds like to eat bird seed, so a bird feeder can also be a good place to see how birds interact with other animals.

Fly-Through Restaurant

1. Use bird field guides or identification books to find out which birds are common in your area. What do these birds eat? Use empty milk cartons or plastic soda bottles to build a bird feeder. Fill your bird feeder and hang it from a low tree limb, a balcony, or a porch. Make sure to keep the feeder full.

Observe your feeder at the same time each day for 30 minutes. Record the number and name of each bird species that you see. Also note any other animals that visit the bird feeder. Write down the behavior you observe between members of the same species and members of different species. Is the behavior you observe the same behavior that is described in the bird identification books? Present your findings as a scientific journal article.

Other Long-Term Project Ideas

INTERNET KEYWORDS
bats
bat house
Bat Conservation International

2. Many people build bird houses, but what about bat houses? Use the library or Internet resources to find out how to build your own bat house. What kinds of bats live in your area? How high off the ground should the house be? What temperature do bats prefer? What color should you paint the house? After you put up the bat house, keep track of how long it takes to attract bats. Present your findings to the class. Why might building a bat house in your area be a good idea?

3. Can you imagine baby-sitting eight children? Eight is the average litter size for a Syrian hamster. Observe a small female mammal, such as a hamster or a mouse, that has recently had babies. For several weeks, take notes on the behavior of the mother and the babies. How do the mother and the babies interact? How do the babies interact with each other? What are their sleeping and eating patterns? How do those patterns change as the babies get older? Share your findings with your classmates in a poster display.

4. Why have Tamarin monkeys been bred successfully in captivity, while other animals have not? Visit a zoo and talk to the scientists about the challenges of creating a successful breeding program. Why are certain species easier to breed in captivity? Make a display that shows 8–10 species of birds and mammals, describes the breeding programs for each, and lists the reasons for the success or failure of each program.

Research Ideas

5. Bobbing and weaving on their long, thin legs, whooping cranes perform an elaborate dance before mating. Why do the cranes dance? Investigate the courtship behaviors of five bird species, and create a poster display comparing the species' courtship behaviors.

6. Over 60 million American buffalo, or bison, once ruled the Great Plains. Today, only about 200,000 bison remain. Research the decline of the bison. What caused it? How were bison important to the Native Americans that lived on the Great Plains? What effect did the decline of bison have on the Native Americans? Write a report that summarizes what you learned.

7. You'd probably go to the hospital if you were bitten by a rattlesnake or a black widow spider, but what if you were bitten by a shrew? The shrew and three other mammals—the platypus, the echidna, and the solendon—are poisonous! Find out more about these mammals. How strong is their poison? How is it used? Write an article about these four poisonous mammals.

8. Warning: Possession of feathers could be a felony. Believe it or not, it is illegal to buy or sell the feathers of some species of birds. Research the laws that control which feathers can be used under what conditions. What kinds of feathers can people legally own? Are exceptions made for certain uses? Why? Create a brochure about the legal and illegal uses of feathers.

9. When you touch or pick up a hibernating Arctic ground squirrel, it won't wake up. But don't try that with a hibernating grizzly bear! Find out more about animals that hibernate. What makes the hibernation of arctic ground squirrels different from the hibernation of bears? What changes occur in an animal's body during hibernation? What other animals hibernate, and why? Write an article about these animals, and explain your findings.

PROJECT
18 **STUDENT WORKSHEET**

DESIGN YOUR OWN

Out of House and Home

LIFE SCIENCE ▲▲▲

If your house suddenly got knocked down where would you go? What happens to the animals that live in the lawn when you mow the grass? When humans build a parking lot, what happens to the plants and animals that made the field or forest their home? Changes to one part of a community can affect all other community members.

SUGGESTED MATERIALS

- metric ruler
- 12 wooden stakes
- hammer
- 6 m of string
- scissors
- permanent marker
- hand trowel

The Plot Thickens

1. Use the following experiment or design your own to investigate what happens when part of a community is changed or removed. Note: Be sure to get permission to use the plot of land.

   In a field, section off three 30 × 30 cm plots of land with stakes and string. Use a permanent marker to indicate plot 1, 2, or 3 on the stakes. Record the plant and animal life found in each plot of land. Indicate the examples of *producers, consumers,* and *decomposers*. In plot 1 remove all the plants and plant roots; in plot 2, cut the plants to a height of 3 cm; leave plot 3 undisturbed. Observe the three plots over a 4- to 6-week period, and record what you see. You may want to take photographs. Compare what happens to the community in each plot of land, and present your findings in the form of a scientific journal article.

Research Ideas

2. Aliens have invaded! What can happen to ecosystems when alien species are introduced, such as cane toads into Australia and kudzu into the United States? Design a "Wanted" poster that alerts the public to the problems caused by an alien species. Include information about a species that is a problem in your area. Include a photo or drawing of the species, information on how it damages the environment, and where the organism comes from. Be sure to include information on efforts to control it.

3. Some species are so important to an ecosystem that the loss of those species can spell disaster for the other organisms living there. Find out what a keystone species is, and identify five potential keystone species in your area. Write a news article explaining the potential environmental impact if one of the species became extinct.

Smokey Says . . .

"Remember, only *you* can prevent forest fires."

For over 50 years, Smokey the Bear's words have reminded Americans to protect forests from fires. You might think that Smokey was created by environmentalists. Actually, he was invented to help the American war effort during World War II. The government needed trees to build ships and airplanes, but trees in the forests were going up in smoke, mostly because of careless people. So Smokey was "born" to make people more careful about fires when visiting forests.

Up in Smoke

1. Forest fires are bad, right? Well, not necessarily. In the early 1990s, drought caused forest fires to rage throughout areas of the Pacific Northwest. Modern firefighting techniques helped to contain these fires. But some ecologists think that forest fires should be allowed to burn unless humans and their homes are threatened. They claim that fires are part of the natural process of succession and renewal. Research both sides of this debate. Which argument do you agree with? Take one position and write a newspaper editorial defending your position.

Other Research Ideas

2. In 1992, Hurricane Andrew blew through southern Dade County, in Florida, and caused a lot of destruction. Investigate the stage of succession that this area has now reached. What plants and animals have returned to the area? Investigate another area that has experienced devastation due to a natural disaster. Compare the current state of succession of this region with the area that was damaged by Hurricane Andrew. Use your research to write a fictional interview with a rock, tree, or river that survived one of the disasters and is watching succession happen.

USEFUL TERMS
primary succession
secondary succession

Long-Term Project Idea

3. If you watch carefully, you might just see succession in action. Find a site that shows signs of primary and secondary succession. Photograph the changes over the course of several months and then create a display exhibiting and discussing the changes.

PROJECT 20   **STUDENT WORKSHEET**

Tropical Medicine

Did you know that 40 percent of modern medicines include an active ingredient that comes from a plant? Digitalis, a medicine used to treat heart conditions, is extracted from an extremely poisonous European plant called foxglove. Because of their biological diversity, tropical rain forests contain untold numbers of plants that could provide treatments and cures for human diseases. Unfortunately, many of the plants in tropical rain forests have not yet been discovered. Therefore, scientists called ethnobotanists are using the help of native peoples to find new sources of medicine, food, and other useful products.

LIFE SCIENCE ▲ ▲ ▲ ▲

INTERNET KEYWORDS
rain forest
medicine
cancer

HELPFUL HINT
If you aren't sure what the natural biome of your region is, you may want to visit a nature center or a state park to find out.

Rx in the Rain Forest

1. Do rain forest trees hold a cancer cure? Research at least five medicines from rain forest plants. How were they discovered? How do native peoples use the plants? How does the human body respond to the plant extracts? What drugs are still in the experimental stages? Share your findings in the form of an article for a health magazine.

Research Ideas

2. Do you live in a desert or grassland biome? a chaparral or temperate deciduous forest biome? Research the biome in your area. What is the climate like? What kind of plants and animals live in the biome? Create an educational Web page or a poster display about your biome. Include pictures of plants and animals, and describe or show what the area looks like during different seasons. Include information about the effects of human activities on the biome.

3. What is a Fynbos or a Nama-Karoo? Believe it or not, each is a different kind of biome. Scientists disagree on the number of biomes that exist. Research a biome not described in your textbook, such as the Fynbos, Nama-Karoo, or sand-sage prairie biome. What species live there? Describe the climate. Compare the definition of this biome to the definition of other biomes in your textbook. Do you think that the biome you researched should be classified as a biome? Why? Present your findings in the form of a research article.

4. During parts of the year, the tundra biome is exposed to darkness 24 hours a day! Research some of the native peoples who live in the tundra. How have they adapted to living in these extreme conditions? For example, how do they protect themselves from the cold? How do they get their food? How do they travel from place to place? Write a story about a day in the life of a tundra dweller.

Name _____ Date _____ Class _____

DESIGN
YOUR OWN

Let's Talk Trash

Banana peels, cardboard boxes, aluminum foil . . . How much garbage are you, personally, responsible for generating? In 1999, each city-dwelling American produced almost a metric ton of garbage. That's right, a *ton*. Do you ever think about where it all goes? Well, about half of it ends up in landfills, which are filling up fast. Recycling can reduce your ton of trash somewhat, but it may not be enough. What else can you do to reduce the amount of garbage you produce each year?

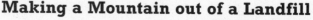

Making a Mountain out of a Landfill

1. Have you ever bought something only to discover that most of the product was packaging? Excess packaging is a major source of solid waste. Think about some of the items you have purchased recently. Choose one company that uses excess packaging for its products, and write that company a letter. Explain that you are working on a school project and would like information about the steps the company is taking to reduce waste in packaging. Include your observations about the company's products, and present suggestions on how the company could reduce waste. Share your letter and the company's response with your class.

INTERNET KEYWORDS
recycling
solid waste management

Research Ideas

2. Many cities have recycling programs, but some of these programs are more successful than others. Research recycling programs around the country, and find out what it takes to run a successful program. What happens at a recycling center? Why are some materials more recyclable than others? Write a report about the more successful programs in the country, and include your suggestions for improving local recycling efforts.

3. Does your city have an air-quality problem? Find out by monitoring daily air-quality reports on the local news or in your local newspaper. What are the health risks associated with air pollution? What can be done to reduce air pollution? Write an article for your school paper about air quality in your community.

4. Did you know that about 50 billion kilograms of the waste produced each year in the United States is considered hazardous to human health? This waste may be flammable, poisonous, radioactive, corrosive, explosive, or infectious. Investigate the effectiveness and safety of current disposal methods for hazardous waste. Create a poster sharing your findings with the class.

Name _____ Date _____ Class _____

DESIGN
YOUR OWN

Mapping the Human Body

How would you make a three-dimensional map of every cubic centimeter of a human body? The scientists working on the National Library of Medicine's *Visible Human Project* figured out an incredible way to do it. The project has produced accurate computer-generated images of two human beings—the *Visible Human Male* and the *Visible Human Female*.

INTERNET KEYWORDS
Visible Human Project
Visible Human Male
Visible Human Female

The Visible Human Project

1. Use the Internet or library resources to find out more about how these models of the human body were created. How will these models be used? Write a science article about the Visible Human Project.

Other Research Ideas

2. Did you know that some amputees feel sensations in their amputated limbs? Research *ghost limb syndrome* or *phantom limb syndrome,* a common condition among amputees. What are the symptoms of this condition? What do doctors and researchers think are the causes of this condition? How can phantom limb syndrome be treated? Present your findings to the class.

3. Did you know that octopuses have three hearts? Why are some organs, such as your kidneys and lungs, duplicated, while others, such as your heart, brain, and liver, are not? Compare human anatomy with the anatomy of two animals that aren't mammals. Make a poster display to illustrate your findings.

Long-Term Projects

4. Surgery once required the use of large incisions and large scalpels, but a type of surgery called *arthroscopic surgery* uses very small incisions and surgical tools that are only 3–4 mm across! Find out more about arthroscopic surgery. What types of injuries is it used for? How effective is it? Interview some people who have had this type of surgery, and write an article about their experiences.

5. Have you ever noticed that some athletes get injured more than others, even though they participate in the same sport? Interview a doctor or other health professional who treats sports-related injuries. Ask about problems that can be avoided by healthy habits and fitness training. Create a pamphlet that outlines some common injuries and ways to prevent them.

Getting to the Heart

Early scientists had unusual ideas about how the human circulatory system works. Some of their ideas were proven inaccurate, while others were proven correct. For example, Galen of Pergamum was a Roman philosopher and physician who lived from A.D. 130–200. Most people in Galen's time believed that the arteries were full of an airlike substance. Galen proved that arteries are full of blood. But he also thought that blood was made by the liver and was "sloshed" through the body.

The English physician William Harvey (1578–1658) was the first to accurately describe the operation of the heart and circulatory system. The popular belief of his day was that the arteries pulsed blood through the body. Harvey demonstrated that the heart, not the arteries, pumps blood through the circulatory system.

Cardiovascular Accomplishments

1. Find out more about the contributions early physicians and scholars made to our understanding of the circulatory system. Were the discoveries of Galen, Avicenna, Andreas Vesalius, Marcello Malpighi, and William Harvey accepted at the time? Write a news article about their work as if you were living at the time in which they did their research.

Other Research Ideas

2. Can you imagine having blood drawn as a treatment for laryngitis? Well, that's what happened to George Washington! For centuries, bloodletting was a standard treatment for many ailments. Research the theory and practice of bloodletting. Why was it used? How did the practice develop? Did bloodletting help patients in any way? Write a historical article about bloodletting.

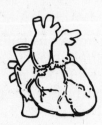

3. If your heart were to stop, could a doctor replace it with an artificial one? Investigate current artificial heart technologies. When must a heart be replaced? What are the challenges to producing a self-contained, artificial heart? What has happened in previous experimental trials? What new experimental technologies are being developed? Write a news article about your findings.

Long-Term Project Idea

4. Would you know what to do if a friend stopped breathing? CPR stands for cardiopulmonary resuscitation, a type of first aid given to a person when he or she stops breathing and has no pulse. What are the basic steps of CPR? What are the requirements for being certified in CPR? Take a CPR training course and receive certification. Create a pamphlet that outlines the information you have learned, and share it with your class.

Name _____ Date _____ Class _____

DESIGN
YOUR OWN

Copying the Kidney

Perseverance can make your dream come true. Dutch doctor Willem Kolff dreamed of finding a way to clean the blood of a patient with kidney failure. As a young assistant at the University of Groningen, Netherlands, Kolff wanted to explore his idea of an artificial kidney, but the chief assistant told Kolff to do as he was told. Kolff didn't give up; he found someone to allow him to work on his idea. At first there were many failures. Some critics argued that an artificial kidney wasn't even needed. But Kolff kept working in spite of what others said. Eventually, he developed a machine that imitated the filtering process of kidneys and saved thousands of lives.

A Machine Imitates Life

1. How does a machine act like a kidney? Research the function and development of kidney dialysis machines. How does a dialysis machine work? Who uses dialysis? How often must dialysis be performed? What recent developments are making it easier for dialysis patients to lead less-interrupted lives? Share your findings in a written report.

Other Research Ideas

2. Both people and cows can eat prairie grass, but the grass is good for cows and bad for people. Research the digestive systems of *ruminants,* animals that chew their cud. How are they able to digest cellulose? How do their digestive systems differ from the digestive systems of humans? Share your findings in the form of a poster project.

3. Can you imagine loving milk but not being able to drink it because it makes you sick? People who are lactose intolerant have trouble digesting milk products. What causes lactose intolerance? How can it be treated? Is there a way for people with lactose intolerance to eat milk products safely? Write a magazine article about lactose intolerance to share your findings.

Long-Term Project Idea

4. Warning: Too much stress may be hazardous to your health! Excessive stress is linked to digestive problems, including ulcers, Crohn's disease, and gastroesophageal reflux. Interview someone who has a stress-related digestive disease. Using reference materials, explore the connection between stress and illness. What changes can people make in their lives to reduce the risk of these diseases? Share what you learned in the form of a magazine article.

Man Versus Machine

On May 11, 1997, an IBM computer named Deep Blue beat the world chess champion, Garry Kasparov, at his own game. Deep Blue's victory was the end of a 50-year battle between human chess players and computers. Does this mean that computers are now smarter than humans? Well, not quite. But it does mean that people are one step closer to making a machine that thinks like a human.

Booting Up Your Gray Matter

1. Artificial intelligence, or the ability of a computer to mimic human thought, has been the goal of many computer engineers since the first digital computer was built. Some scientists, though, think artificial intelligence is impossible since a computer is not like a brain. Write a paper explaining why you think a human brain is or isn't a type of biological computer.

Other Research Ideas

2. What's your brain up to when you are "catching your Zs?" Does it take a nap as well? Does it try to calculate the value of pi? Or does it just play "mind games"? Instead of sleeping on it, go to your library and learn more about your nightly brain activity. Present your findings on a poster.

3. "Go laskt and get a poziuy." Would you know what to do if you heard this command? That sentence is similar to what a person suffering from aphasia would hear if you asked him to go out and get a pizza. Research a brain disorder, like aphasia or epilepsy. What are the symptoms of the disorder? How are they treated? Write an article about the disorder. Include an example or a specific case.

Long-Term Project Ideas

4. Do you know anything newsworthy about nerves? Create a magazine called the *Daily Dendrite* about the brain and nervous system. Include factual articles, pictures with captions, cartoons, advertisements, and an interview with a fictitious brain surgeon or a victim of brain damage. Present what you have researched about the nervous system using a wide variety of creative techniques.

5. How well could you get along without your senses? Design an experiment to see how people who can't use one of their senses, such as sight, hearing, or touch, complete normal daily tasks. Make sure your teacher approves your experiment before you carry it out.

PROJECT

26 **STUDENT WORKSHEET**

DESIGN
YOUR OWN

LIFE SCIENCE

Get a Whiff of This!

Does love have its own smell? The male gypsy moth thinks it does. This little guy can sniff out a female gypsy moth kilometers away because of the pheromones she gives off. Pheromones are chemicals animals use to communicate with other animals of the same species. Without pheromones, gypsy moths wouldn't be able to find mates. But what about humans? Do people use pheromones to attract the opposite sex?

Whatcha Got in Your Nose?

1. How would you go about sniffing pheromones? Well, you would need to use a structure called a vomeronasal organ, or VNO. For centuries, anatomists have insisted humans don't have VNOs. But recently scientists took another look. Sure enough, they found an organ that looked like a VNO tucked up in people's snouts. Does this mean human reproduction could be influenced by pheromones? Use library resources to explore this question. Write a report supporting your position.

Other Research Ideas

2. Do you know a language? Of course you do. Learning a spoken language is a major part of human development. But how do we do it? Investigate how humans learn languages, and present your findings orally to your class.

3. You wouldn't be here if it weren't for hormones. Hormones play a big part in reproduction. If a woman doesn't have the correct balance of sex hormones, she can't ovulate. Likewise, a man with a hormonal imbalance may have trouble producing healthy sperm. Unfortunately, chemicals that can mess up human hormone cycles are being pumped into the environment every day. These chemicals are a lot like estrogen, the primary female sex hormone. Use the Internet to learn more about environmental estrogens and present your findings on a poster.

Long-Term Project Idea

4. One baby, two babies, three babies—four?! Fertility treatments have started a wave of multiple births in the United States. This "multiplication of multiples" has been greeted with open arms by many families, but how do the parents cope? After all, taking care of one baby at a time is hard enough, much less taking care of two or three babies. Interview the parents of twins, triplets, or more to find out how they handled their baby boom. Write an article about your findings.

HELPFUL HINT

The study of language is called *linguistics*. The ability to learn a language is called *language acquisition*.

INTERNET KEYWORDS

environmental estrogens

endocrine disruptors

EDSTAC

HELPFUL HINT

If you can't find these busy parents in your home town, try the Internet, and then conduct your interview on-line.

PROJECT
27 **STUDENT WORKSHEET**

A Chuckle a Day Keeps the Doctor Away

Has your doctor ever prescribed laughter to cure your cold? Probably not, but maybe he or she should. As many people have suspected for years, your physical health and emotional health are closely related. That means the happier you are, the healthier you are. So cheer up and put a smile on that face—your life may depend on it!

It's All in Your Head

1. Friends are good for a lot of things, but what do they have to do with fighting off the sniffles? Stanford University psychiatrist David Spiegel thinks your friends can save your life—or at least prolong it. In a 1989 study, he showed that cancer patients in support groups survived an average of 17 months longer than patients not in support groups. Make a video about how good emotional health can help you ward off disease.

Another Long-Term Project Idea

2. Ask your parents or your doctor which vaccines you've been given. When were you given each vaccination? The vaccines should have initials, like MMR. Find out what the letters in each vaccine stand for. For example, MMR stands for Measles, Mumps, and Rubella. Research the diseases that the vaccines protect you against. What are the symptoms of the diseases? Are the diseases very common now? Create a poster display about the different vaccinations and the diseases they prevent.

Research Ideas

HELPFUL HINT
The first modern biological weapons were developed by the Japanese government during World War II.

3. Can something microscopic be used as a weapon? You bet it can. Many countries develop tiny killing machines—viruses, fungi, and bacteria—to be used in warfare. They are called biological weapons. Research the history of biological weapons, including ways people have defended themselves against them. Present your findings in a paper.

4. What can cure diseases, clean houses, purify food, save crops, and more? Antibiotics! Yet, antibiotics are becoming less and less effective against bacteria. Find out how bacteria become resistant to antibiotics and research possible solutions to this problem. Present your findings orally to your classmates.

PROJECT
28 | **STUDENT WORKSHEET**

DESIGN
YOUR OWN

Breakfast, Lunch, and Dinner of Champions

As you wait for the signal, you can feel the butterflies in your stomach. Your heart is racing; the crowd is starting to go wild. Before you take another breath, the starting shot is fired, and you take off on your bicycle.

Being able to compete as an athlete takes a lot of discipline and training, as well as mental and physical endurance—but that's not all. The food you put into your body affects how you feel and how much energy you have. If you were a professional athlete, you probably would need to follow a specific diet to give yourself maximum energy.

LIFE SCIENCE

Eating for the Gold

1. How does an athlete get the energy he or she needs? Find out how much energy we use for our body processes, such as breathing. Research the additional energy it takes to play a particular sport and the number of hours per day a professional athlete usually trains for that sport. Then research various foods and design a diet for an athlete in training. Keep in mind that a professional athlete may have different nutrient requirements than a less-active person has. Make a video detailing the best foods and diet for an athlete in training.

Research Ideas

INTERNET KEYWORD

fluoridation

2. What does your drinking water have in common with toothpaste? Fluoride! Fluoride is added to drinking water to help protect your teeth from cavities. There is still a controversy surrounding this practice. Why is fluoride added to drinking water? How much fluoride is added? Why do some people think fluoride should not be added to drinking water? What evidence supports adding or not adding fluoride? What do you think? Write a position paper supporting your view.

3. SURGEON GENERAL'S WARNING: "Smoking Causes Lung Cancer, Heart Disease, Emphysema, and May Complicate Pregnancy." Cigarette manufacturers are required by law to print warning labels, such as the one above, on all cigarette packages and advertisements. Why did the Surgeon General recommend these warnings on cigarettes? What evidence is there that smoking causes health problems? Research the history of cigarette warning labels and the trend toward limiting the places where smoking is allowed. Write an essay about the history of smoking in the United States.

PROJECT
29 **STUDENT WORKSHEET**

How Big Is the Earth?

Eratosthenes was a Greek philosopher who lived from about 276 to 196 B.C. Using simple materials, he managed to make an accurate measurement of the circumference of the Earth. All he needed was a stick, a little geometry, and two important assumptions: the Earth is round, and the sun's rays are parallel.

SUGGESTED MATERIALS
• stick
• protractor
• atlas or globe

This Experiment Is Well-Rounded

1. Research the life and work of Eratosthenes. Then make your own measurement of the circumference of the Earth. Use the suggested materials at left to try this experiment. Follow the scientific method in Chapter 1 of the text to design your experiment. Consider the following questions after you complete your experiment: How was your experiment the same as Eratosthenes'? Did you get results similar to his? Write a paper about the experiment and the effects of Eratosthenes' discoveries on the scientific and nonscientific communities.

Another Long-Term Project Idea

2. Research the life and work of a famous scientist. Find out about the culture in which the scientist lived, personal accounts of the scientist's life, and the scientist's research. With a partner, write a script for a fictional interview between the scientist and a journalist. The interview should be 5–10 minutes long. If possible, include safe demonstrations of the important scientific ideas. You may want to dress in costume and videotape your interview. Present your interview to the class or to younger students.

Name	Occupation
Florence Bascom	geologist
Edward D. Cope	paleontologist
Pierre de Fermat	mathematician/astronomer
Galileo Galilei	astronomer/physicist
Grove Karl Gilbert	geologist
Maria M. Winkelmann Kirch	astronomer
Isabel Lewis	astronomer
Othniel Marsh	paleontologist
Maria Mitchell	astronomer
Caterina Scarpellini	meteorologist/astronomer
Alfred L. Wegener	geologist

Name _____ Date _____ Class _____

DESIGN
YOUR OWN

Globe Trotting

Your friend Aaron de Vurld has invited you on a trip. He'll take you anywhere you want to go, but you have to do *all* the planning. Aaron is also a bit picky; he likes to have very detailed plans—including time schedules and maps—before going anywhere. Where would you like to go?

Hit the Road!

1. Use library resources to research and plan your trip with Aaron. Choose at least four cities on different continents. Write a detailed trip schedule that outlines what you'll see in each city, and attach a map of the route you will take. Include the mileage, estimated arrival and departure times, and means of transportation for each leg of the journey. Don't forget about time zones, and be sure to factor in enough time to enjoy the sights!

Other Research Ideas

INTERNET KEYWORDS
time zone
Greenwich Mean Time
standard time

2. Dinner at 8 . . . A.M.?! That could happen if people around the globe set their watches to the same time. Use library and Internet resources to research the history of time zones. How were travel schedules made before time zones were standardized? What problems did travelers have? Who wanted time zones standardized, and why? How are they standardized today? Present your findings in the form of an oral or written report.

INTERNET KEYWORDS
cartographer
cartography
mapmaking
Al-Khwarizmi

3. How would you make a map without any knowledge of latitude? Some early cartographers—people who make maps—didn't know how to calculate latitude. To get around this problem, Al-Khwarizmi, a ninth-century Islamic cartographer, calculated the position of the sun at the summer solstice. Use Internet and library resources to research the cartography methods of Al-Khwarizmi and other early cartographers. Then create a poster that displays each method and explains why it did or did not work.

Long-Term Project Idea

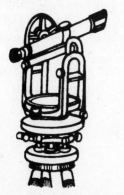

4. Surveying is a centuries-old profession. In fact, George Washington spent his early career as a surveyor! Many modern surveyors map topography, but some surveyors even map archaeological digs. Learn about basic surveying techniques. You might contact a transportation department or a civil engineering firm for help. Ask if you can accompany a team on assignment. Compare the team's measurements with those on a map of the area. Share what you've learned in a presentation.

EARTH SCIENCE ▲▲▲

Name _____ Date _____ Class _____

What's Yours Is Mined

What minerals have you used today? Did you drink from a soda can? Did you read the time on a quartz watch? Are you wearing a gemstone ring? If so, you've relied on mineral resources, such as aluminum, quartz, and gold. Mineral resources are mined from ore deposits in the ground. In surface mining, soil and rock are stripped away to expose the ore underneath. Surface mining is often the fastest and cheapest way to extract the ore, but it is also the most damaging to the environment.

INTERNET KEYWORDS
surface mining
strip mining
land reclamation

Mining for Information

1. The Surface Mining Control and Reclamation Act of 1977 requires mining companies to restore a surface-mined site to its original condition. Visit a reclaimed site, and compare the restored area to the undisturbed, surrounding area. You might want to document your visit with a videocamera. Also, look up the official definition of *reclaimed area*. Does the site satisfy the definition? In your opinion, how effective was the reclamation? Find out what happens when an area isn't properly reclaimed. Present your findings and conclusions in the form of a special news report to the class.

Another Long-Term Project Idea

2. How does a diamond become part of a ring? Learn how jewelry is made. Interview a jeweler about the criteria used to classify gemstones and determine their quality. Prepare a set of questions such as the following: What tools are used? How are different gems and metals handled? How does a diamond cutter decide where to cut? Why are opals cut without facets? Are specific jewelry settings required for certain gemstones? Use pictures and illustrations to present your findings to your classmates.

INTERNET KEYWORDS
piezo-electric effect
piezo effect
quartz clock

Research Idea

3. Why is quartz used in so many electronic devices, such as radios, televisions, watches, and computers? What is the "piezo-electric effect," and how does it work? What elements and conditions are needed for the effect to be useful in electronics? Use Internet and library resources to find out the answers to these and some of your own questions. Then take apart an old (working) quartz clock, and observe the inner workings. Share what you learn with your classmates.

PROJECT
32 **STUDENT WORKSHEET**

DESIGN YOUR OWN

Home-Grown Crystals

Peter Roque: Hello, and welcome to this week's edition of *In Your Garden*. Today we're interviewing that world-famous gardener Ms. Mary Contrary. So, Mary, how *does* your garden grow?

Mary: My garden grows best with table salt, ammonia, charcoal . . .

Peter Roque: Wait a minute! What kind of flowers are you growing?

Mary: Flowers? I'm not growing flowers. I'm growing a *crystal* garden. With the right procedure, my household ingredients will become a beautiful stack of crystals. I can even change their appearance by changing their growing environment!

MATERIALS

- tray
- 2 small, disposable plastic or plastic-foam bowls
- 150 g of charcoal
- 5 mL teaspoon
- water
- table salt
- ammonia
- laundry bluing
- food coloring (3 different colors)
- dishwashing gloves

Grow Your Own Crystal Garden

1. Use the materials listed at left, and follow the steps below to make a colorful crystal garden. Document your crystal growth with daily sketches or photos.

Day 1: Put on the dishwashing gloves. Put all the charcoal in one bowl. Sprinkle 15 mL of water, 15 mL of salt, and 15 mL of laundry bluing over the charcoal. Do not stir.

Add several drops of food coloring to this mixture. Do not stir. Leave the bowl overnight in a place where it will remain undisturbed.

Day 2: Sprinkle 15 mL of salt over the mixture.

Day 3: In the second bowl, mix a solution of 15 mL each of salt, laundry bluing, water, and ammonia. Pour the solution around, not over, the charcoal in the first bowl.

Check the progress of your crystals daily. When crystal formation slows, repeat the step for Day 3. You may repeat this step as many times as you wish to create more crystals.

Consider the following questions:

- How do your crystals differ from naturally formed crystals?
- Can you make the crystals grow faster? How?
- How does the growing surface affect crystal growth?
- Can you get the crystals to grow at different angles?

Make a poster display of your findings. Be sure to include your photos or sketches.

EARTH SCIENCE

Home-Grown Crystals, continued

Another Long-Term Project

2. Have you ever thought about writing a book for younger children? Write and illustrate a children's book about the rock cycle. You might consider writing the story from the point of view of a grain of sand. Look at children's science books in your local library for ideas about how to explain difficult terms to younger children. Arrange to read your story to a class of elementary-school students. Be prepared to answer any questions they may have concerning the information you present.

Research Ideas

3. Have you ever broken apart a rock to discover crystals inside? Were you surprised? A geode is a plain-looking, round stone that is lined with crystals. Use resources in your library and on the Internet to find out about geodes. How do they form? What causes the formation of different crystals? Why are crystals different colors? Where are geodes most likely to be found? Present your findings to the class using pictures, drawings, or actual samples.

4. The marble in the mountains around Carrara, Italy, is very white. The color of the marble is due to the lack of organic material in the limestone from which it crystallized. Carrara marble has been mined for 5,000 years. The marble was used in the interior of the Roman Pantheon; the Leaning Tower of Pisa; St. Peter's Basilica, in Rome; and in the Kennedy Center for the Performing Arts, in Washington, D.C. Research how marble is formed and how the different colors and veins in the marble are produced. Is there special care that must be taken with the marble? Prepare a display that shows your findings.

PROJECT
33 **STUDENT WORKSHEET**

DESIGN YOUR OWN

Build a City—Save a World!

It *is* possible to protect the environment and still have modern conveniences like electricity. Residents of Gaviotas, Colombia, are planting trees and using renewable energy sources, such as the sun and wind, to supply the community with electricity. The people of Arcosanti, Arizona, used the concept of *arcology*—a blend of ecology and architecture—to build a self-sufficient city that is in harmony with the environment. Also, civil engineers are beginning to plan for *sustainable communities*—communities that can expand without causing permanent damage to ecosystems.

INTERNET KEYWORDS

arcology

Arcosanti

eco-city

sustainable community

sustainable development

Plan an Eco-City

1. Use Internet and library resources to research the design of "eco-cities" and sustainable communities. Find out how they produce, use, and conserve energy. What are the advantages and disadvantages of these cities? What works well in these cities? What doesn't work well? Design and build a model of an eco-city or a sustainable community. Include a guide to the eco-friendly features of your design.

Other Long-Term Project Ideas

2. Have you ever wondered where the objects all around you came from? Interview a representative from a local steel mill, foundry, or computer microchip factory to learn how the business converts raw materials into finished products. What raw materials are needed to create their products? Create a poster that tracks the path of raw materials from the factory to the consumer.

INTERNET KEYWORD

Energy Efficiency and Renewable Energy Clearinghouse (EEREC)

3. How energy-efficient is your school? Interview an energy expert from the Energy Efficiency and Renewable Energy Clearinghouse (EEREC) about energy-efficient and renewable-energy technologies. Use library and Internet resources to research these technologies, and then draft a proposal for using these technologies in your school.

USEFUL TERM

cogeneration
a process in which two usable forms of energy are produced from a single fuel source

Research Ideas

4. What if you could use fuel to produce electrical energy *and* produce another, usable form of energy? That's what cogeneration is all about! One example is the use of heat released in a manufacturing process to boil water that drives a steam generator. Research other examples of cogeneration. How could cogeneration be used in other industries? How could it save money and fuel? Write a magazine article about what you have learned.

EARTH SCIENCE

PROJECT
34 **STUDENT WORKSHEET**

The Hard Rock Chronicles

Have you ever wondered how scientists know so much about dinosaurs, even though dinosaurs have been extinct for 65 million years? We know what dinosaurs looked like, what they ate, even who their friends were—all from some pieces of old rock! Paleontologists can learn a lot from the right rock. They use clues from fossils and other rocks to determine how long-dead organisms might have looked and acted. So where are fossils to be found? And how do paleontologists know where to dig? Believe it or not, fossils can be found almost anywhere, even in your own backyard!

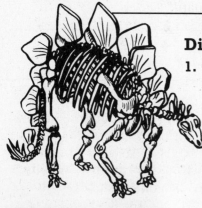

Dig It!

1. Are you a rock fan? Find out more about fossils by visiting a museum of natural history in your city or on the Internet. Interview the museum curator or tour guide. Where did the museum get its fossils? How are fossils formed? What kind of information can a paleontologist get from a fossil? How are broken pieces of fossils reassembled? Write a report, create a Web page, or make a video documentary to present what you've learned.

INTERNET KEYWORD
La Brea Tar Pits

Other Research Ideas

2. Can you imagine falling into a pool of black, sticky tar? Well, it has happened to plenty of creatures over the centuries in what is now the heart of Los Angeles, California. The La Brea Tar Pits have been a valuable source of fossils for paleontologists for about 100 years. Research the La Brea Tar Pits, and find out what paleontologists have learned from them. How are the fossils removed from the pits? What kinds of organisms have been discovered? When did they fall into the pits? Present your research in the form of a magazine article.

3. Where did humans come from? How do we know? We have learned much about the evolution of humans from various fossil sources. What have scientists recently learned about our early human ancestors? Has any new evidence caused scientists to reevaluate and revise older theories? Present your findings in the form of a news article.

Long-Term Project Idea

4. Contact a local paleontologist to arrange a visit to a fossil dig in progress for you and a few classmates. What is the age of the rocks at the dig site? What techniques are used to uncover and protect fossil finds? What question is the paleontologist hoping to answer by excavating the site? Be prepared to make several visits to the area over several weeks. Document and report your findings with pictures and a written report or with a documentary video.

PROJECT
35

STUDENT WORKSHEET

Legend Has It . . .

According to Irish legend, two giants—Finn McCool of Ireland and Finn Gall of Scotland—were feuding. In order to sneak up on his foe, Finn McCool built a bridge out of huge stone columns, which spanned the great distance between his land and Finn Gall's. Tired from the effort, McCool went home to rest before the great battle. Finn Gall, having discovered the bridge, arrived at his enemy's home demanding to see McCool. McCool's clever wife pointed to her husband and said that only she and her sleeping baby were home. Finn Gall thought to himself, "If this huge thing is the baby, the father must be gargantuan!" Not wishing to fight such an enormous rival, Finn Gall raced home over the bridge, destroying it as he went. All that is left of the bridge are its two ends: the Giant's Causeway, in Northern Ireland, and Fingal's Cave, in Scotland.

INTERNET KEYWORDS
columnar jointing
basalt column

The Science Behind the Myth

1. The Giant's Causeway and Fingal's Cave are two locations where dramatic basalt columns have formed. Basalt columns are large, hexagonal, blue-gray towers that are formed when hot lava cools and cracks. Find out more about these amazing formations. Where else are they found? Demonstrate what you learned by building a model of a basalt column for the class. Explain how plate tectonics led to the formation of basalt columns.

Research Ideas

2. As scientists find out more about the Earth, they develop new theories about its changing surface. Go to the library, and investigate how geologists explained earthquakes and volcanoes in the past. Look in encyclopedias or magazines from the 1940s up to the present day. Compare older theories with modern ones. How have they changed? What are the problems with the older explanations? Make a chart that compares the explanations from the different time periods. Be sure to include illustrations.

3. Where do scientists predict the position of the continents will be in 50 million years? Pick one continent, and determine what effects the continent's future position will have on its climate and ecosystems. What direction do scientists believe the continental plate is moving? How will that effect the climate? Will today's species of plants and animals be able to survive? Present your findings in the form of a map that shows the climatic changes that you expect to occur in the next 50 million years.

EARTH SCIENCE

Name _____ Date _____ Class _____

A Whole Lotta Shakin'

Every 30 seconds or so an earthquake occurs somewhere in the world. That's about 1 million earthquakes per year. So why hasn't every major city been leveled? Well, fortunately, most earthquakes occur beneath the ocean and are so slight that humans cannot feel the effects. However, once every 2 to 3 years a major earthquake occurs, often resulting in a huge loss of life and property. Even as our knowledge of earthquakes increases, we still have many questions about their causes and how we can prevent property damage and the loss of human life.

INTERNET KEYWORDS

California Earthquake Data Center

National Earthquake Information Service

National Earthquake Information Center

Public Seismic Network

Whose Fault Is It?

1. Use the Internet to monitor earthquake activity in California or another earthquake-prone area over a 9-week period. Gather data from the California Earthquake Data Center or the National Earthquake Information Service by visiting its Web site every few days. Plot each earthquake on a map of the area, and look for a pattern in the earthquake activity. Locate the San Andreas Fault or the fault that is near the earthquakes. Present your findings to the class.

Another Long-Term Project Idea

2. What if the Earth were kept afloat in a vast sea by a giant catfish? Every time the catfish flipped over, the Earth would move. That's how the ancient Japanese explained earthquakes. Research how earthquakes were explained by ancient philosophers, such as Aristotle, and by myths and folklore of different cultures, such as Chinese, Scandinavian, or Native American cultures. What was the purpose of these explanations? Did the purpose of ancient explanations differ from the purpose of modern explanations? Compare the explanations with the theories of modern science. Then present your findings in the form of a play or a skit.

Research Idea

3. There are many ways to measure the size of an earthquake. Research the Modified Mercalli Intensity scale, moment magnitude, and the Richter scale, and create a chart that compares them. Find information, including firsthand accounts, about two or three recent earthquakes. Use your chart to evaluate the size of the earthquakes. Then create a display that uses graphs to compare the earthquakes according to these scales. Which of these scales do you think is the most useful? Why?

PROJECT
37 **STUDENT WORKSHEET**

DESIGN YOUR OWN

A City Lost and Found

In A.D. 79, Mount Vesuvius erupted in a volcanic display of ash, fire, smoke, and lava. In the aftermath, cities at the foot of the volcano were almost completely buried under 3 m of volcanic debris and more than 6 m of volcanic ash. Nearly 17 centuries later, workers discovered remains in an underground tunnel from one of the buried cities. Through careful excavation, the ancient Roman city of Pompeii has emerged. Preserved beneath volcanic ash, Pompeii provides a glimpse of what life was like before Mount Vesuvius erupted. By examining the ruins, tools, and artwork, scientists have developed a picture of what the people of Pompeii wore, what they ate, and how they lived.

The Final Act

1. Research the eruption of Mount Vesuvius and the destruction of Pompeii. Find out who Pliny the Younger was and why he was important. Also, investigate how everything in Pompeii was so well preserved. Write a play about the last days of life in Pompeii, and perform it for your class. Include an accurate account of the eruption.

Another Long-Term Project Idea

2. Visit a volcano. Many places in the national park system feature volcanic-rock formations or active volcanoes. Visit or find out more about one of the parks. Is the volcano active or extinct? What rock formations are unique to that particular site? What effects has volcanic activity had on the surrounding areas? Videotape the park and present your findings by narrating the video. Or, obtain a topological map of the area and build a 3-D model of the park, labeling the areas that have been affected by volcanic activity.

Research Ideas

3. A large volcanic eruption can cause changes in climate. How does this happen? How long do these climatic changes last? Choose an eruption, and gather climatic data for the area before and after the eruption. Plot your findings on a map.

4. The eruption of Mount St. Helens in 1980 devastated an area of 500 km^2, destroying many of the plants and wildlife in the area. What were the short-term and long-term effects of the eruption on the humans, animals, and plants of the region? How are the plants and animals recovering? Write a newspaper article explaining the changes in the area from the time of the eruption to the present.

EARTH SCIENCE

DESIGN
YOUR OWN

Precious Soil

You step on it. You stomp on it. You walk all over it. Soil doesn't seem very precious. But it is. Without soil, which is a mixture of weathered rock and humus, there would be no plants. Without plants, we would have no food to eat and no oxygen to breathe. Soil is *very* precious to our way of living. Some people spend their entire careers studying soil. Why don't you give it a try?

SUGGESTED MATERIALS

- 100 mL of each soil sample
- soil pH test kit
- tall cylindrical glass jar with lid
- distilled water
- ruler

SAFETY ALERT!

Remember to treat your earthworms, like all other animals, with respect and care.

Getting the Dirt on Soil

1. Conduct a soil-sample exchange with two or three other schools. Test the soil samples for pH and composition. For the composition test, fill the jar half full with soil (record the volume of soil). Add distilled water until the jar is three-quarters full. Screw the lid on tightly and shake it until all of the soil particles are suspended in the water. Set the jar aside and allow the soil to settle. The heaviest particles in the soil will sink first and the lightest particles will sink last. You will be left with bands of soil of different particle sizes. Measure the width of each band and the radius of the jar. Find the volume of each layer using the formula: volume = 3.14 × radius × radius × width. Then calculate the percentage of each soil component in the soil sample. Identify the soil particles in each band. Exchange the information you have gathered with other schools.

Another Long-Term Project Idea

2. Earthworms may be wiggly, but they are very useful critters. As they burrow through the ground, they aerate the soil and eat organic matter, turning it into plant food. Research earthworms and earthworm farming. How many kinds of earthworms are there? Which types can you find in your area? Build your own earthworm farm. You can either order your worms or collect them around your neighborhood. What conditions will keep your worms healthy? Experiment to find out what foods your earthworms prefer. What don't they eat? You can also collect the worm castings and use them as fertilizer. Create a brochure for interested worm farmers.

Research Idea

3. Do you still think dirt is dirt? Well, scientists classify soils into 10 distinct orders. Research the different soil types. What are their names? Decide which you have in your region. Verify your local soil types by looking at a map of soil types in an atlas, such as *Goode's World Atlas*. Use what you have learned to create a brochure for potential gardeners in your area.

Canyon Controversy

The effects of the Glen Canyon Dam on the Colorado River are controversial. When the dam was built in the early 1960s, it changed the natural flow of the river. Before the dam was built, the Colorado River flooded every spring, clearing the river of sediment and providing water and nutrients to the plants and animals living on the river banks. The dam stopped the flooding, and the organisms that depended on the floods started to die off. In an effort to restore the river ecosystem, scientists are using the dam to produce controlled flooding in the spring.

INTERNET KEYWORDS
Glen Canyon Dam
Colorado River Management

Debating the Dam

1. Research the Glen Canyon Dam controversy on the Internet. Form a group to debate the proposal to tear down the dam. Each group member should choose one of the following roles: a representative from a local water-management agency, scientist, dam construction worker, or environmental activist. All group members should research their viewpoint and be able to support their argument.

Other Research Ideas

2. Every couple hundred years the Mississippi River *avulses*—it abandons its existing delta to form a new one. Research how some cities might be affected if a river changes course. Find out when the river last changed its course. When can the river be expected to change course again? What can the cities do to be ready? Write a news story explaining the phenomenon to the residents along the river, and describe what the city should do.

3. An aquifer can be a town's most important natural resource. Research an aquifer in or near your community. How large is the aquifer? What type of rock is the aquifer composed of? Mark the aquifer and its recharge zone on a map. How is it recharged? Indicate its natural outlets on the map. How might the quality of water in the aquifer be threatened? Present your findings on a poster that persuades people to help take care of the aquifer.

Long-Term Project Idea

4. How is the water in your community? Contact your local water board and have a water analysis sent to you. If your water quality is poor, get involved in a water-quality monitoring project or a water cleanup project in your area. Write an article that explainsthe quality of your water supply and what is being done—or should be done—to improve the quality.

HELPFUL HINT
For help finding a project in your area, you might want to contact your local government, a local environmental group, or the Environmental Protection Agency (EPA).

EARTH SCIENCE

Deep in the Mud

You are a member of the local chapter of the Society of Swift Water Awareness and Mud Prevention. This morning you received the following urgent message from the Society of SWAMP:

Our town is washing away! We must take action. The long summer drought killed most of the grass in the community, leaving only exposed soil. Now the heavy rain is causing mudslides everywhere—with one exception. For some reason, the soil is staying in place in the botanical gardens. We need your help to find out how to stop the erosion, or soon our town will be sliding down the river.

SUGGESTED MATERIALS

- native plant seeds
- garden gloves
- trowel
- field guide
- string
- hose

Slip Sliding Away

1. Select a rapidly eroding patch of land near your school as a restoration site, and get permission from the owner to restore the area. Alternatively, contact someone in your local parks department to see if they're willing to set aside a small area for you to conduct your restoration activities. Use a field guide to identify several of the native plants near the site. Do the following steps in order:

   a. Mark off the restoration site with string.

   b. Hang signs identifying the area as a "Land Restoration Area."

   c. Determine the type of soil in your area and the amount of sunlight that the area receives daily. Buy native plant seeds that are best suited for those conditions. You may want to conduct your restoration in the spring so that you can grow wildflowers.

   d. Plant the seeds according to the instructions on the package.

   e. For 10 days, visit your test site daily, and make sure that the soil receives enough water for the seeds to germinate.

   f. After 10 days, visit your site once a week for the next 6 weeks, carefully recording the progress of your restoration.

   How effective was your land restoration project? Did any problems develop? How did you solve those problems? If you did this project again, what would you do differently? Create a display with photographs of your project in various stages of development to show the progress of your restoration.

Deep in the Mud, continued

Other Long-Term Project Ideas

2. Flooding causes serious problems in some areas. If possible, view a documentary on floods and flooding to get some background material on the subject. Your local library may have some relevant documentaries. Then, make a list of questions about flood control projects in your area. Using E-mail or a phone, conduct an interview with a representative from the Army Corps of Engineers or FEMA. After you learn about the projects, make a model of some of the techniques used locally.

3. Ice-age glaciers dramatically changed the face of the Earth. The geographies of Cape Cod, Massachusetts, and Long Island, New York, are examples of such glacial activity. Research the ice-age formation of this area. What are the geographical features there called? How did the area look before the glaciers receded at the end of the ice age? How are Cape Cod and Long Island still changing today? Build a model that shows how Cape Cod or Long Island was formed by glaciers.

Research Idea

4. Erosion affects many types of human activity—from farming and landscaping to architecture and city planning. What types of erosion affect your community? Find areas in your community where erosion has occurred. Compare these areas with areas that have been protected by erosion-prevention techniques. Present what your findings in a poster display.

EARTH SCIENCE

▲
▲▲
▲

PROJECT
41 **STUDENT WORKSHEET**

DESIGN
YOUR OWN!

Your Very Own Underwater Theme Park

You and your friends think it's high time someone built an underwater theme park. And who better to plan it but yourself? You pay a visit to your friend, Moe Kneebaggs, for some advice on how to embark on such a business venture. He recommends that you take a lot of care in choosing the perfect site for such a park. Picking a location that is in shallow water can save you a lot of money during construction. You have a topographic map of the ocean floor, but how will you find the *actual* depth of the water?

The Final Global Frontier

1. Just as the land is made of rolling hills and valleys, the surface of the ocean is made up of *liquid* hills and valleys. The ocean's surface level can vary in height by as much as 150 m! The *TOPEX/Poseidon* satellite is part of NASA's mission to carry out oceanographic research from space. What kind of data is collected by the satellite? How has this data led to a greater understanding of the oceans? Write a paper that describes your findings.

Other Research Ideas

2. Would you spend a hard day at work for a lump of salt? Roman soldiers did; they were often paid in salt. In fact, the word *salary* means "money from salt." How has salt affected world trade and culture? Where did ancient cultures find salt? Prepare a poster that illustrates the different methods of collection and the uses of salt throughout history.

3. Are tidal plants the solution to the global energy problem? In St. Malo, France, and Murmansk, Russia, tidal plants have been generating electricity from ocean tides since the late 1960s. Investigate how a tidal plant works. Where else are these plants being used? How efficient are they? What new technologies are being developed to make the use of tidal plants more widespread? Make a pamphlet that explains the costs and benefits of tidal power.

Long-Term Project Idea

4. They're fighting about fish? Research the debate over fish population counts. How are fish counted? Why is there disagreement among fishermen and scientists over fish population counts? Interview a fisherman or an ecologist about fish populations. How do scientists determine if a fish population is endangered? What effects do fish counts have on the fishing industry? Choose a position and write an opinion paper about the topic.

PROJECT
42 **STUDENT WORKSHEET**

DESIGN YOUR OWN

An Ocean Commotion

The mad scientist rubs his hands together and gives an evil laugh. "Soon, I will change the weather, and the world will be mine! Ha-ha-ha-ha-ha."

Science fiction is full of stories of mad scientists trying to control the world by changing the weather. But Mother Nature has her own way of dramatically changing global weather patterns. She does it through a shift in ocean currents that meteorologists call El Niño

INTERNET KEYWORDS
El Niño
fisheries
fishing industry
fish population

Something's Fishy

1. Does El Niño affect whether you can have fish for dinner? The fishing industry is dependent on ocean conditions and fish populations. Find out on the Internet or in the library how El Niño affects the populations of ocean fishes, fisheries, fishermen who depend on the ocean for their livelihood, and the availability of fish at the market. Share your findings in the form of a newspaper article.

Other Research Ideas

2. Catch a wave, and you might feel like you're on top of the world. Research the connection between waves and surfing. What kinds of waves do surfers look for? What makes a great surfing wave? How are different waves approached? Which part of a wave does a surfer ride? Why? What conditions do experienced surfers avoid? Why? What are the dangers of surfing? Share your findings with the class in the form of a poster presentation.

3. Ocean water is always moving, but where does it go? In the 1990s, several countries participated in the World Ocean Circulation Experiment to map global ocean currents. Which countries participated in the project? What were the goals of the project? Find out about the methods scientists used to map ocean currents. For example, the Global Drifter Center at NOAA/AOML tracks buoys that float along with the ocean currents. How did the scientists gather their information, and what conclusions were drawn? Present your findings in the form of a science article.

Long-Term Project Idea

4. Would you know what to do if a tsunami was on its way to your town? Many people live in low-lying coastal areas that some day could be threatened by a tsunami. Find out what steps to take before, during, and after a tsunami. If you live along the coast, are there evacuation routes laid out? Create a video about tsunamis and explain what people can do to protect themselves from a tsunami's destructive power.

EARTH SCIENCE ▲▲▲

PROJECT
43 **STUDENT WORKSHEET**

DESIGN YOUR OWN

A Breath of Fresh Ether?

At one time, some people believed that the Earth's atmosphere was part of a substance that filled all space—even beyond the moon and the planets of our solar system. The substance was called ether. In 1887, physicists A. A. Michelson and E. W. Morley conducted an experiment that produced astonishing results and finally showed that this kind of ether did not exist.

INTERNET KEYWORDS
Michelson-Morley
Albert Einstein

A Brilliant Failure

1. The Michelson-Morley experiment has been called the most brilliant failure in scientific history. What was the experiment? How did the two scientists prove that ether did not exist? How were the results of the experiment explained at the time? How did Albert Einstein later explain the results? Write a newspaper story about the experiment as if you were reporting it as it happened.

Other Research Ideas

2. How did sailors cross the ocean before engines? Early explorers used only wind. How were global winds mapped before the use of modern technologies? Find out the routes Christopher Columbus, Ferdinand Magellan, and Vasco da Gama used to cross the ocean. Draw a map showing the routes and the winds these early travelers used to make their journeys.

INTERNET KEYWORDS
sick building syndrome (SBS)
building-related illness (BRI)

3. Can a building make you sick? Researchers for the Environmental Protection Agency and the National Institute for Occupational Safety and Health found that indoor pollutant concentrations are generally 10 to 100 times higher than outdoor concentrations. Surprisingly, this is only a recent phenomenon. What causes sick building syndrome? Why has it become more common in the last 20 years? How can it affect your health, and what can be done about it? Write an article for a medical newsletter sharing your findings.

Long-Term Project Idea

SAFETY HINTS
• Avoid exposure from 10 A.M. to 2 P.M. when the sun's rays are most intense.
• Drink lots of fluids.
• Do not stay in the sun more than 2 hours. If you notice any discoloration, get out of the sun immediately.

4. Trying to avoid a sunburn from those dangerous UV rays? Why are UV rays harmful? How do you know which tanning lotion to use? Do all lotions with the same SPF give you the same protection? Does a higher SPF number mean more protection? Find out by conducting an experiment to test 10 different tanning lotions in a variety of brands and SPF values of 8 and above. Share your findings in the form of a poster presentation to the class.

PROJECT

44 **STUDENT WORKSHEET**

DESIGN YOUR OWN

A Storm on the Horizon

The animals are acting strange. The horses are skittish and the dogs are running in circles. They can sense that the calm of this afternoon will soon be shattered by a devastating storm. The wind will howl, sheets of rain will pound, trees will bend and snap under the force of 190 km/h winds. Hurricanes are some of the largest and deadliest storms on Earth. Fortunately, with modern detection techniques such as radar and satellites, humans have fair warning before these mighty storms hit.

Be Prepared

1. What kinds of severe weather affect your community? How can you prepare yourself for severe weather? Find someone who has witnessed a dramatic storm. Interview him or her about the experience. Ask what happened, what he or she learned from the experience, and what advice he or she would give to others. Make a video documentary of your interview.

Another Long-Term Project Idea

2. How do ski lodges use dry ice to make artificial snow? How does artificial snow differ from natural snow? Build a model of an artificial snow maker, and demonstrate to the class how artificial snow is formed.

Research Ideas

3. There is nothing small about microbursts. These sudden, localized bursts of wind can knock over trees and tear the roof off a house in minutes. Find out more about microbursts. Under what conditions do they form? What technology is being developed to detect microbursts? Make a poster to display your findings, including a diagram illustrating microburst formation.

4. Some physical features of the Earth generate more clouds than others, allowing people to navigate by observing clouds. For example, Native Americans could locate the Mississippi River from great distances because the river was a natural cloud generator. Research natural cloud generators and find out how they have helped travelers. Write a science feature article about your research.

5. Australian aborigines predicted rain by measuring the amount of moisture in seaweed. What did other cultures use to predict the weather in ancient times? Make a poster that displays the methods that different cultures have used to predict the weather.

EARTH SCIENCE

PROJECT
45 **STUDENT WORKSHEET**

Sun-Starved in Fairbanks

It's New Year's Day in Fairbanks, Alaska. The stars shine brightly in the dark morning sky. It's 9 A.M., but the sun won't rise for at least another 2 hours! At a chilly –23°C, it's too cold and dry to make a snowball! In fact, most people just stay inside, drink hot chocolate, and dream about summertime.

INTERNET KEYWORDS
Season Affective Disorder (SAD)

The Winter Blues

1. What would it be like to have no sunshine, or near-constant sunshine? Find out about a condition called Seasonal Affective Disorder, or SAD, that some people who live in polar regions suffer from. Use library or Internet resources to explore how people cope with the effects of excessive darkness or sunlight. Then create a video of a television program in Fairbanks, Alaska, advising newcomers on how to live comfortably during extended periods of sunlight and darkness.

INTERNET KEYWORDS
Iditarod
dog sled
mushers

Research Ideas

2. The Iditarod—Alaskans call it the "Last Great Race on Earth." Each year, 60 brave women and men attempt this incredible 1,833 km dog sled journey from Anchorage to Nome. What is it? The word *Iditarod* comes from the Athabascan Indian word meaning "the distant place." Research the Iditarod on the Internet. How do race participants, referred to as *mushers,* prepare for the conditions they will encounter across the taiga and the Arctic tundra? And how do mushers and their dogs survive the 2- to 3-week adventure? Make a "how-to" guide for surviving and finishing the Iditarod.

3. Why would a large group of people suddenly uproot and move to another continent? Climatic changes may have influenced the migrations of Mongoloid peoples from Siberia across the Bering Land Bridge to North America. Research the migration of these peoples, the Paleo-Indians. What do scientists know about their migrations? What evidence is there that the migration was related to changes in climate? What adjustments, if any, would the people have had to make? Imagine you are a Paleo-Indian and write a firsthand account that describes the reasons for the trip and your arrival in North America.

PROJECT
46 **STUDENT WORKSHEET**

DESIGN YOUR OWN

Celestial Inspiration

Why did we start studying the stars? Many scholars believe that astronomy was first used to time the planting and harvesting of crops, thousands of years ago. When constructing the pyramids, ancient Egyptians used an astronomical instrument called a *merkhet* to align the pyramids almost perfectly with the four cardinal directions. And the regularity of celestial events, such as the consistent movement of the stars across the night sky, made it possible for the Egyptians and Mayans to develop sophisticated, accurate calendars.

INTERNET KEYWORDS
Egyptian astronomy
Pyramids of Khufu
Egyptian calendar

Ancient Investigation

1. Find out more about ancient Egyptian astronomy. Find examples of early calendars, star or navigational charts, or astronomical buildings. How do these examples differ from modern versions? What information did the early Egyptians model most correctly? How did the ancient astronomers come to their conclusions? Write a scientific article to describe your findings.

Other Research Ideas

2. Each year many satellites are launched into orbit above the Earth. They are used for a variety of purposes, such as communications, weather forecasting, and defense. Choose one satellite currently orbiting the Earth and answer questions such as the following: What kinds of energy waves has the satellite collected? What things in the universe emit these waves? What information have scientists been able to gather from the satellite? Share your findings in the format of a newspaper article.

3. How many moons has it been since you looked at a lunar-based calendar? There are a number of alternative calendars still in use that are lunar-based. Investigate calendars used by other cultures. Compare how and why the different calendars were created, and compare the advantages and disadvantages of using a lunar-based calendar. Prepare a display comparing the different calendar systems.

Long-Term Project Idea

4. The time is . . . half past a stick! Before modern clocks were invented, people used a device called a *sundial* to measure the time. Build your own sundial. Don't forget to consider daylight savings time, true North, and latitude and longitude. How do each of these variables affect your sundial reading? Give an oral report of your discoveries to the class, and demonstrate how to use your sundial.

EARTH SCIENCE

A Two-Sun Solar System?

It's late on a Saturday night and you and a friend are watching a science fiction movie on television. It's your favorite part, when the hero finds himself stranded in a desert after his ship has crashed on a distant planet. Without water he may never make it to the nearest scientific outpost. The blazing sun hangs high overhead, hurting his eyes and burning his parched lips. Suddenly he sees a second sun rising. Our hero is doomed! The heat from the second sun will surely seal his fate.

A Star Is Born

1. A solar system with two suns?! Is that possible? Some people believe that in the dawning of our solar system Jupiter almost became a star. Find out why Jupiter is sometimes called a "failed star" or a "near sun." What are the characteristics of a star? What are brown dwarfs? What would have had to happen during the formation of our solar system in order for Jupiter to become a star? Could this still happen? Pretend that you and a partner are film critics who are reviewing the movie scene described above. Videotape a show in which you debate whether this scene could actually take place in our solar system.

Research Ideas

2. Solar wind particles can disturb the Earth's ionosphere. A strong solar wind can disturb the Earth's magnetic field, interfering with radio and television transmissions as well as microwave communications. A strong solar wind can also endanger astronauts in space. What are solar winds? What causes them? What problems do they cause for some technologies, and why? Make a poster display of your findings.

3. Are there clues about Mars on Earth? Research how information on the changing composition of Earth's atmosphere might help scientists understand the history of other planets. What is the atmosphere of Mars like now? What was the composition of its original atmosphere? Write an article about your findings.

4. Meteorites give us clues about the formation of the solar system. By using radiometric dating methods, scientists have determined the age of all meteorites to be about 4.5 billion years, about the same age as Earth. What are some scientific theories explaining this phenomenon? Write a report on the competing theories. Decide which one you support and explain why.

DESIGN YOUR OWN

What Did You See, Mr. Messier?

Imagine that you are outside on a clear night observing the sky through a telescope. Suddenly, you notice a bright, fuzzy object that appears to have a tail of light coming from one side. Are your eyes playing tricks on you, or have you just found a comet? How can you tell? Well, you might start by checking the Messier Catalogue. The Messier Catalogue is a list of 109 celestial bodies compiled by Charles Messier, an eighteenth century astronomer and comet chaser. Messier compiled this catalogue of objects that could be mistaken for comets in order to make comet hunting easier.

INTERNET KEYWORDS
Messier Catalogue
comets
Charles Messier

Look Up!

1. Find out more about Charles Messier and the Messier Catalogue in the library and on the Internet. What types of celestial bodies are included in the Messier Catalogue? Why are these celestial bodies likely to be confused with comets? Visit an area at night that does not have light interference, and identify as many Messier objects as you can. Create a guide to help others find and identify these objects.

Another Research Idea

2. Many Near Earth Objects (NEOs) have crashed into Earth. What clues did these objects leave behind? Investigate the physical and environmental impact of NEOs. Explain how scientists use crater information to determine the size, mass, and speed of the NEO that made the crater. Describe your results in a scientific article.

Long-Term Project Ideas

HELPFUL HINT

The eight phases of the moon are the following: new moon, waxing crescent moon, first quarter moon, waxing gibbous moon, full moon, waning gibbous moon, third quarter moon, and waning crescent moon.

3. Have you ever really looked at the moon? Observe the moon every night for at least 2 months, and keep a moon journal. Try to make your observations from the same place and at the same time each night. Use binoculars to make observations. Sketch the moon, and describe its color, shape, position in the sky, and phase. Present your observations on a poster. Be sure to include illustrations.

4. Many meteor showers and comet appearances are predictable. For example, Halley's comet passes by the Earth every 76 to 77 years. Find out the date of the next meteor shower or appearance of a comet. Observe the event, and record your observations. Why do comets pass by the Earth periodically? Investigate the sightings of Halley's comet over the last 2,000 years. How did ancient astronomers predict the occurrence of this comet? Write a magazine article about your observations and research.

EARTH SCIENCE

PROJECT
49 **STUDENT WORKSHEET**

Contacting the Aliens

If you could communicate with aliens, what would you tell them about our species? In 1974, we sent a message traveling at light speed toward the stars of the Hercules constellation. The message was sent from a large radio telescope in Arecibo, Puerto Rico. Scientists hope that the message, which bears information about humans and Earth, will be intercepted by intelligent extraterrestrial life. That is, if there is such a thing . . .

USEFUL TERM

exobiology
the investigation of the possibility of extraterrestrial life

Is Anybody out There?

1. Research the possibility of life elsewhere in the universe. What are the conditions necessary for life? What is the likelihood of the existence of extraterrestrial life? What calculations have exobiologists made to determine the probability of life on distant planets? What other attempts have been made to contact intelligent extraterrestrial life? Give an oral presentation to your class on the subject of exobiology. Be sure to include visual aids.

Other Research Ideas

2. Some galaxies are speeding away from the Earth at 1 million meters per second! Why don't the stars look like they're moving that fast? Find out how scientists know that other galaxies are moving away from ours. What kind of data led scientists to develop the big bang theory? How do scientists determine what direction a galaxy is moving? What is red-shift and blue-shift? How is the Doppler effect involved? Create a computer or poster presentation to share your research.

3. What is your favorite constellation? Find out about the stars in this constellation. Determine the name of each star, its apparent and absolute magnitudes, surface temperature, class, and distance from the Earth. What was each star named for? Make a poster display of your research. Include an H-R diagram of each star in the constellation.

Long-Term Project Idea

4. How much of science fiction is science and how much is fiction? Watch a science fiction movie or read a science fiction novel about space or space travel. Take careful notes when the characters discuss cosmology and astronomy. Compare the science presented in the story line with what you have learned in class and researched. How accurately does the book or movie portray scientific information? How do the fictional explanations for cosmological events compare to current findings in astronomy? Present your findings in a book review or movie review.

PROJECT
50 **STUDENT WORKSHEET**

DESIGN
YOUR OWN!

Space Voyage

Imagine that you are the lead scientist planning a space expedition to Proxima Centauri, the nearest star to the sun. You must do a lot of research on the current technology that is available to your crew. You've spent months working with engineers and space travel experts designing the equipment and plotting the course. But, before the crew can make such a huge trek, you must prepare them for it.

The Lead Scientist Speaks

1. Plan this trip using what is currently known about space and space travel. Where is Proxima Centauri? How long will the trip to Proxima Centauri take? (Don't forget that faster-than-light travel is impossible.) What kind of equipment will the crew need for a successful expedition? Prepare a lecture for the crew before they take off. What will they need to know about the trip? Videotape the lecture and share it with your class.

Research Ideas

2. Space exploration and the use of satellites have littered Earth's orbit with "space junk." How much space junk is orbiting the Earth? Does it interfere with satellite operations or with shuttle missions? Is this debris hazardous? Does anyone keep track of it? What steps are being taken to reduce the accumulation of space junk? Write about your findings in a science article.

3. What do Tang® and dehydrated ice cream have in common? Both were developed for astronauts! Find out about five commonly used products that were developed for the space program. Prepare a display showing the original purpose and the new uses of each invention.

4. Research what people living in the 1950s thought the space program would be like in the future. Which of the technologies they predicted are actually used today? What expectations didn't come to pass? Use primary sources, such as newspaper and magazine accounts. Write a humorous report of your findings.

5. You may have heard of Gregarin, Glenn, and Armstrong. But what about Laika, Enos, and Ham? They were space pioneers too. But they weren't human. Find out about the animals used in the early days of the American and Russian space programs. What kinds of animals were sent into space? What resulted from the animal missions? Write an imaginary travel journal from the perspective of one of these animals.

EARTH SCIENCE

HELPFUL HINT

Popular Science and *Popular Mechanics* might be particularly helpful.

PROJECT
51 **STUDENT WORKSHEET**

DESIGN
YOUR OWN

Prove It!

In the late 1700s, some scientists believed that water could be turned to earth if it was boiled. To prove this, they took a glass container full of water and boiled it for several days. When all the water had boiled off, a residue remained. They believed that this residue was earth. Antoine Lavoisier, a French chemist, guessed otherwise.

He conducted the experiment again, but this time he weighed the glass container, the water, and the residue before and after boiling. He collected all of the water that was boiled off and found that it had the same weight as the water did before it was boiled. He also found that the weight of the residue and the container after boiling equaled the weight of the container before boiling. He concluded that the residue must not be from the water, but from the glass container! It was, in fact, tiny bits of matter that came off the glass as the water was heated. Using the scientific method, Lavoisier proved that water does not turn to earth.

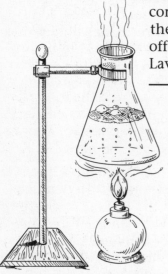

A Hot Debate

1. Find out more about the work of Antoine Lavoisier. What kinds of experiments did he perform? Choose one of Lavoisier's experiments and research the history behind it. What was he trying to disprove? How did Lavoisier's method differ from his opponents' methods? Write a script for a debate that he might have had with one of his opponents about the experiment. Include how he used the scientific method to come to his conclusions. With a partner, perform the debate for your class.

Another Long-Term Project Idea

2. What is it like to be a physical scientist? Research the life and work of a famous physical scientist. Describe how he or she contributed to the scientific knowledge of the time. With a partner, write a script for a 5–10 minute fictional interview between the scientist and a journalist. Include one or two simple and safe demonstrations of the important scientific ideas. Videotape your interview and show it to the class or to younger grades.

A Research Idea

3. How do you build a model that doesn't take up any space? Use a computer, of course! Recent advances in computer-modeling techniques have helped researchers better understand everything from nuclear explosions to experimental surgical techniques. Research the exciting advances in computer modeling and simulation. Present your findings in the form of a magazine article.

SUGGESTED SCIENTISTS
• Niels Bohr
• George Washington Carver
• Marie Curie
• Albert Einstein
• Dorothy Crowfoot Hodgkin
• Maria Goeppert Mayer
• Sir Isaac Newton
• Blaise Pascal
• Norbert Rillieux
• Chien Shiung Wu

DESIGN
YOUR OWN

And We Have Thales To Thank

Thales of Miletus (585 B.C.) was a Greek philosopher and a very inquisitive fellow. Thales asked the question, "What is the world really made of?" After careful thought, he concluded that all the matter in the world originated from water! Thales was wrong, but by asking questions about the origin and properties of matter, he provided an early foundation for our modern scientific method.

A Philosophical Matter

1. Other Greek philosophers, such as Anaximedes (525 B.C.), Heraclitus (500 B.C.), and Aristotle (350 B.C.), had their own theories about matter. Find out how these philosophers classified matter and which properties of matter they described. For example, according to Aristotle's system, how would you describe an apple? How did each philosopher develop his theory? How is each theory different from modern theories of matter? Write a play centered around a discussion these philosophers might have had if they all participated in one debate about the nature of matter.

Another Research Idea

2. The space shuttle is protected by an outer covering of ceramic tiles with certain physical properties. What are these properties? What factors did the engineers consider when designing the tiles for the shuttle? How could the ceramic tiles be improved? What other uses do you think this ceramic would have on Earth? Write an article describing your findings.

Long-Term Project Idea

3. Have you ever wondered why some toasters have a metal covering and some have a plastic one? Go to a junk shop or second-hand store, and purchase an old countertop appliance, such as a toaster, coffee maker, or blender. Take it apart and try to determine what material each of its parts is made of. List the physical and chemical properties of these materials. You may need to measure some of the properties yourself or look them up in a reference book. Why do you think the appliance is made out of materials with those properties? You might want to consider things such as: durability, practicality, consumer interest, and manufacturing cost. Make a chart that summarizes the properties of each material and the benefits of using it in this appliance.

> **HELPFUL HINT**
> Some useful properties of matter are color, reactivity, strength, heat conductivity, malleability, ductility, and density.

> **SAFETY ALERT**
> Be sure the appliance is unplugged before you take it apart.

PHYSICAL SCIENCE

PROJECT
53 **STUDENT WORKSHEET**

Episode IV: Sam and His Elephants Get That Sinking Feeling

As we join Safari Sam and his band of faithful companions, the evil Captain Blunder is busy hatching a plan to bring about poor Sam's demise. Sam and his elephants faithfully make their way past the swamp only to fall into a giant quicksand trap set by the evil captain. Needless to say, Sam and his elephants are taken by surprise. Does quicksand spell the end of Safari Sam? Will Sam and his elephants make a narrow escape? Join us next time for the exciting conclusion to "The Continuing Tale of Safari Sam."

Quicksand!

1. When sand, clay, and water are mixed in a certain way, quicksand is formed. Undisturbed, quicksand appears to be solid. But when the quicksand is disturbed, it behaves like a liquid. The phenomenon is known as thixotropy. Research more about quicksand and thixotropy. Does thixotropy occur with any other substances? Use your findings to write the final episode of Safari Sam's adventures. Be sure to include any information you have found in your research. Videotape a performance of your script, and show it to your class.

Research Ideas

2. What do a campfire, a lighting bolt, and a lit fluorescent tube have in common? They are all made up of plasma, which are states of matter composed of electrically charged particles. Nuclear fusion, which occurs in the sun and may be a source of energy in the future, occurs in plasmas. Research other examples of plasmas. Under what conditions do they form? Make a poster displaying the properties of plasmas and some technologies that use them.

3. A snowflake is a fascinating example of a transition of matter from gas to solid. Did you know that some snowflakes can be as large as 10–15 cm in diameter? How do snowflakes form? How does temperature affect the shape of snowflakes? Create a poster display that illustrates and describes some snowflake shapes and how they form.

4. Did you know that Grandma's brownies might not turn out so tasty if she baked them on Mount Everest? As altitude increases, the boiling points of liquids decreases. So cooking at higher altitudes requires different recipes. Find a high-altitude cookbook, and compare the recipes with those in a normal cookbook. Present your findings in the form of a magazine article.

USEFUL TERM

deposition
the transition of matter from the gas state to the solid state

---

A Coin-cidence?

Since civilization began, gold, silver, and copper have been three of the most precious elements. Wars have been fought over these metals. People have spent their lives searching for the gleam of gold or the shine of silver hidden in a wall of ordinary rock. What is it about these three elements that makes them so precious?

Precious Knowledge

1. What properties do copper, silver, and gold have in common? How are they different? Why is gold more valuable than copper or silver? Historically, what have been the uses for gold, silver, and copper? What modern uses do these three elements have? Prepare a display highlighting the properties and uses of these elements.

2. What does the *K* in 14K gold stand for? It stands for *karat*, a measure of gold purity. Gold used in jewelry usually contains other metals, such as silver or zinc. A combination of metals is called an *alloy*. Research alloys of gold. What other metals are used to form gold alloys? How do the properties of these alloys compare with the properties of pure gold? How do metal workers decide which metals to combine and what proportions to use? What new alloys are being investigated, and why? Write a report of your findings.

Another Research Idea

3. It wiggles. It jiggles. It tastes good. Fruity gelatin—what *is* it made of? Gelatin is one example of a colloid. Find out more about this jiggly substance. How is it made? What is it made of? What makes it a colloid? You know it is used in food, but what other industries use gelatin? Create a poster that displays your findings.

Long-Term Project Idea

4. Proper separation of mixtures is very important in the oil, water, and mining industries. Interview a representative from an oil company, mining company, or water-treatment plant about the separation techniques that are used in the industry. What substances are separated? What properties do those substances have? How do the separation techniques take advantage of those properties? Write a magazine article about the details of your interview.

INTERNET KEYWORDS

element + gold
gold alloys

EARTH SCIENCE ▲▲▲▲

Name _____ Date _____ Class _____

Tiny Troubles

The evil Dr. Minnie Mizer has shrunk you to the size of a small mouse with her incredible shrink ray! She's left you on her desk, which is too high for you to climb down. The nearest piece of furniture is a bookshelf 25 cm away. On the shelf is a lamp with a cord that you are pretty certain you can climb down. You could easily escape if you could just reach that lamp. But, you are unable to make such a long jump. The only things on the desktop are a small bottle of glue and several boxes of toothpicks. Suddenly, you have an idea. If you can use the glue and the toothpicks to build a bridge across the gaping chasm, you could flee to safety. You better hurry, because Dr. Mizer's cat, Snacker, may show up any minute now!

Toothpick Task Force

1. Balanced forces are very important when it comes to bridge designs. Research how different kinds of bridges are made. What forces do engineers consider when designing a bridge? Build a bridge with toothpicks and glue. You may use craft sticks instead of toothpicks. The bridge should span 25 cm and should be strong enough to hold your textbook. For a challenge, hold a contest to see whose bridge can support the most weight.

Another Long-Term Project Idea

2. Design and construct a model of a motorless car that will move in a straight line. The car should accelerate to top speed by traveling down a ramp, and must continue traveling a distance of 3 m on a smooth surface. Build your car from scrap materials, like the materials listed at left. Calculate the speed of your car over a fixed distance and average it over three trials. Where should friction be minimized on the car? What materials can be used to reduce friction? Where does the force of friction help the car move faster? What materials can be used to increase friction? How does mass affect the car? How does the angle of the ramp affect the car's speed? Demonstrate for the class what your car can do. Be sure to explain which features of the car allow it to reach top speed.

Research Idea

3. You know that you use a scale to measure weight and a balance to measure mass. But, how are scales and balances constructed? What measurements are used in association with them? How do various types of scales and balances differ? Why are some types of scales or balances considered more reliable than others? Make a poster displaying what you have learned.

SUGGESTED MATERIALS

- aluminum foil
- bamboo skewers
- drinking straws
- glue
- rubber bands
- masking tape
- plastic film canister lids
- jar lids
- sand paper
- tongue depressors

DESIGN YOUR OWN

"Any Color You Want, so Long as It's Black"

When the Model T Ford rolled off the production lines in 1914, it was offered in only one color—black. Black paint dried much faster than other colors, so Henry Ford's car factories could make more automobiles in less time by painting their cars black. Ford was famously quoted as saying that you could get a Ford in "any color you want, so long as it's black." It wasn't until 1926 that the Model T was offered in other colors. Think of all the colors that cars come in today! The roads today are filled with cars of every color from black to lime green. Cars have changed a lot since 1914 and in more exciting ways than just the color of their paint.

And Away We Go

1. Cars are always changing! Research the changes made in the design of automobiles over the last century. Do these changes make cars safer, faster, or more fuel efficient? Think of two new design changes that could improve the safety or efficiency of a car. Create a poster display with pictures of the car and illustrations of your new design elements. Also include explanations of the changes' benefits on your poster.

Another Research Idea

2. A Major League Baseball pitcher can throw a ball at 150 km/h (93 mph). Can you imagine how much energy it would take to make a ball travel 20 times faster than that? Well, scientists are working on a device called a *ram accelerator* that could accelerate objects to hypervelocity—speeds much faster than the speed of sound. In a ram accelerator, a huge force acts on the small mass of the projectile to achieve rapid acceleration. How does a ram accelerator work? What generates the huge force that acts on the projectile? What are the potential uses for a ram accelerator? Write an article about the development of the ram accelerator and its potential uses.

Long-Term Project Idea

3. Interview a race car driver, bicycle racer, or stunt driver about how speed, acceleration, and momentum affect them in their line of work. Also ask them about the effects of gravity and friction on vehicle movement. Videotape or tape-record your interview. Present your recording, along with simple demonstrations, to a younger class to teach them about the forces of motion.

PHYSICAL SCIENCE

DESIGN YOUR OWN

Scuba Dive

You take a deep breath, adjust your mask, put your regulator in your mouth, and tip over backward off the boat. With a splash, you enter the warm, blue water. Your own breathing sounds loud in your ears as you descend slowly. Brilliantly colored tropical fish swim past you, your ears clear, and you find yourself at home in the world beneath the waves.

Under the Sea

1. Many forces relating to water limit undersea exploration. Research the sport of scuba diving. What equipment was used before the invention of scuba gear? When was scuba gear invented? Find out what changes have been made since scuba diving first came about. What are the properties of fluids that can make diving hazardous? Write an article for your school newspaper about the science behind scuba. Using your research and what you know about forces in fluids explain the precautions scuba divers must take to ensure a safe dive. Be sure to include a description of the health risks of diving to great depths and how divers control their buoyancy.

Another Research Idea

2. The first submarines were little more than hollowed-out iron cylinders. After World War II, great advances were made in submarine technology. What kinds of materials are used in submarines today? How are modern submarines different from the early submarines? How are submarines designed to withstand the pressures of deep sea submersion? How are submarines designed to take advantage of forces in the water? Make a poster of different submarine designs or a cut-away model of a sub and present your research to the class.

Long-Term Project Idea

3. Until 1999, many people attempted to go around the world in a hot air balloon, and all of them failed. What made the difference in 1999? What kinds of hot air balloons were being used? What were the most common problems faced by would-be *circumnavigators*, people who travel around the world? When were hot air balloons first invented? How have balloon designs changed over the years? Design a new hot air balloon, and create a marketing brochure to attract a fictional sponsor. In the brochure, you will need to point out the strengths of your design and explain why it is better than previous balloons that failed.

PROJECT

58 **STUDENT WORKSHEET**

DESIGN YOUR OWN

To Complicate Things

Rube Goldberg was a cartoonist famous for drawing elaborate, complicated machines that accomplished simple tasks. His work was so unique and well liked that his name is used to describe all machines that are similar to the ones he drew. There are even contests to see who can design and build the most elaborate Rube Goldberg machines. A good Rube Goldberg machine uses many complex steps to complete a task that would normally take only one or two steps. For instance, a machine designed to turn on a light switch might involve rolling bowling balls, burning candles, jumping frogs, popping rubber bands, and spilling water. The more complicated Rube Goldberg machines are, the better.

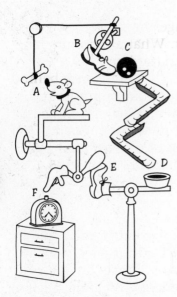

Don't Keep It Simple

1. Build your own Rube Goldberg machine that lifts a shoe at least 30 cm, waters a plant, turns off an alarm clock, or performs another simple action. Be creative in your choice of materials, but be sure they are not flammable or hazardous. The machine should perform at least five steps to accomplish its task. Try to keep your machine compact—it shouldn't be bigger than 1 m³. Use as many simple machines as you can in your Rube Goldberg machine. Compete with your classmates to see who can be the most creative and use the most steps.

Another Long-Term Project Idea

2. Wind power is one of the most promising sources of pollution-free energy for the future. Research windmill designs that have been used throughout history in different parts of the world. Build models of different windmills, and find out which designs work best for certain tasks. Consider the following questions: How have windmill designs changed? Where and how are windmills being used today? Write this information on note cards, and attach them to your models.

Research Idea

3. Did you know that some bicycles built in the 1800s had wooden wheels and iron tires? These bikes were so uncomfortable to ride that they were called "bone-shakers." Research the history of the bicycle. What were the early bicycle designs? When was the first "modern" bicycle built? What variations have there been on the modern bicycle? How could current bicycle designs be improved? Draw a series of diagrams of bicycles, from the earliest models through today's models. Include your design for the "bike of the future."

PHYSICAL SCIENCE

Name _____ Date _____ Class _____

DESIGN YOUR OWN

Great Balls of Fire

While sitting on her front porch during a thunderstorm in 1985, a Massachusetts woman saw a "white ball of fire" rolling up her street. It was sparking and crackling and sending out small fingers of lightning to the cars and telephone poles it passed. The ball, about a meter in diameter, split into three pieces, then into six, then joined back to three, and then back to its original size before disappearing. The power in the neighborhood went out for $2\frac{1}{2}$ hours.

   Seem strange? Most people have witnessed lightning bolts in thunderstorms, but few have ever seen ball lightning. Although rare, it has been noted by individuals all the way back to the ancient Greeks. Ball lightning has been reported to enter airplanes and even to "chase" a flight attendant around the cabin! The nature of ball lightning is not well understood, ranking it among the more interesting scientific mysteries of the day.

INTERNET KEYWORD
ball lightning

A Striking Idea

1. Using the library and the Internet, find out more about ball lightning. How often is it reported? What are some theories to explain it? Are there any myths about ball lightning? Write a report in the form of a scientific magazine article. If possible, include quotes from firsthand reports of its sightings.

Another Research Idea

2. Where will the energy your children use come from? Though we rely on fossil fuels for the majority of our energy today, their limited supply and environmental impact force us to keep seeking new ways to generate energy. What are the most promising alternative energy sources being explored today? Choose one technology and create a Web page or report about it. Include its advantages and disadvantages, its potential for large-scale use, and a brief history of its development.

Long-Term Project Idea

3. Is your refrigerator taking money from you? Is your dishwasher sapping precious energy? Some appliances use more energy than others to do the same amount of work. Visit an appliance store, choose one type of appliance, and record the information shown on the yellow Energy Guide tag (the estimated cost of using that appliance for one year) for each model of that appliance. Make a chart listing several appliances in one category from highest to lowest Energy Guide rating. What features might lower the Energy Guide rating for the appliance you chose? Prepare a report of your findings.

STUDENT WORKSHEET

DESIGN YOUR OWN

Firewalking Exposed

Randolph Atkinson eyed the glowing pit of red coals that lay before him. His bare feet twitched in anticipation. "Am I crazy?" he asked himself. "Why am I doing this?" Before his doubts got the better of him, he took a deep breath and stepped forward. His mind raced. "I'm walking on fire! I can't believe this!"

Believe it. Firewalking is real. The earliest stories of firewalking probably came from India around 1200 B.C. Since then, it has been an organized event in many different cultures and religions. In the 1930s, scientists began paying closer attention to this phenomenon and began to study how it is possible to walk across a bed of hot coals (around 425°C!) without burning one's feet. In the interest of science, some of these scientists even took the walk of fire themselves!

SAFETY ALERT!

You shouldn't do this at home! Firewalking requires expert knowledge and preparation.

INTERNET KEYWORD

firewalking

Hot Stuff

1. Using the library and the Internet, investigate the history and physics of firewalking. How has it been explained in other cultures? What is science's explanation for why firewalking is possible? Are there any tricks that firewalkers use to protect their feet from the hot coals? Present your research in the form of a magazine article or web page.

Another Research Idea

2. Nature knows best! Animals have developed several different adaptations to gather, conserve, and get rid of heat. For example, the hair of a caribou, or reindeer, is hollow. Caribou live in very cold climates, and the hollow hair traps air and provides good insulation. Choose an animal that lives in either a very hot or a very cold climate, and research its adaptations for dealing with the extreme temperatures. Make a poster display with illustrations to explain your animal's adaptations.

Long-Term Project

3. Humans have been experimenting with their own ways of dealing with body heat. Investigate the relative warmth of several different fabrics. Why are some fabrics better insulators than others? Which materials stay warm when they are wet? Which do not stay warm when they are wet, and why? Are synthetic materials better insulators than natural ones? Devise an experiment to find out how well different fabrics insulate. Be sure to include fabrics used in cold-weather hiking or camping gear. Create a brochure that explains the properties and the best uses of different fabrics.

PHYSICAL SCIENCE

PROJECT
61 **STUDENT WORKSHEET**

DESIGN YOUR OWN

How Low Can They Go?

The never-ending quest to better understand our universe has led scientists to some amazing places, from the deep reaches of outer space to the heart of the atom. Our curiosity has shown us things smaller than anyone thought existed—first the atom and then subatomic particles. But scientists didn't stop with protons, electrons, and neutrons. Instead, they devised sophisticated instruments called particle accelerators to take a close look at subatomic particles. What they found were even smaller subatomic particles, which they named quarks, positrons, and gluons. Will they keep looking for something even smaller? Of course!

The Quirks of Quarks

1. Find out more about subatomic particles like quarks. How many different kinds of quarks are there? Where do quarks fit into the atomic model? Do they carry a charge? What is their mass? Write a scientific magazine article and build a model of the subatomic particle you researched.

INTERNET KEYWORDS
cyclotron
particle accelerator

Other Research Ideas

2. How do you dig into a nucleus? Find out about particle accelerators and cyclotrons in your library and on the Internet. How do they work? How many particle accelerators or cyclotrons exist in the United States? in the world? When was the first particle accelerator built? How big are they? Write a newspaper article to report your findings.

3. How does a TV work? Television sets use cathode ray tubes to create a moving picture. How do cathode ray tubes work? What other items besides television sets use cathode ray tubes? A new generation of television sets that are not much thicker than a picture frame are now on the market. Do they use cathode ray tubes or some other technology? Present your findings to the class in an oral presentation with visual aids.

Long-Term Project Idea

4. Arrange a tour of a commercial chemistry lab, environmental chemistry lab, or the chemistry department at a university. What instruments are used in the lab to identify atoms and compounds? What is the purpose of each instrument? Find out the primary fields of research being explored in that lab. If you have a camera, take pictures. Write an article describing your tour for the school paper.

PROJECT
62 **STUDENT WORKSHEET**

DESIGN YOUR OWN

It's Element-ary

The history of the periodic table is like a detective story that spans many centuries. Although most of the elements on Earth have been around for billions of years, scientists have had to do some sleuthing to find each element's unique identity.

The ancient Greeks knew nine elements, including gold, sulfur, copper, and carbon. These elements, which are found in almost pure form as minerals, are called *native elements*. In 1669, Hennig Brand was the first scientist to actively search for and isolate an element. It was phosphorus. After that, many other scientists looked for other elements. In fact, seventy-four other elements were discovered between 1737 (cobalt) and 1925 (rhenium). The contributions of history's "elemental" detectives have helped build the modern periodic table—a chemist's best friend.

John Dalton's Table of Elements, 1808

ELEMENTS

		W				
⊙	Hydrogen	1	⊕	Strontian	46
◐	Azote	5	⊖	Barytes	68
●	Carbon	5	Ⓘ	Iron	50
○	Oxygen	7	Ⓩ	Zinc	56
⊘	Phosphorus	9	©	Copper	56
⊕	Sulphur	13	Ⓛ	Lead	90
◑	Magnesia	20	Ⓢ	Silver	190
⊖	Lime	24	⊛	Gold	190
◍	Soda	28	Ⓟ	Platina	190
◍	Potash	42	⊙	Mercury	167

HELPFUL HINT

Try searching for the name of the metal, plus the word *toxicity*, *poisoning*, or *elemental*. For example, you might search for *cadmium toxicity* or *lead poisoning*.

Periodic Changes

1. Find older versions of the periodic table in textbooks and encyclopedias from the last 75 years. How has the periodic table changed? How is it the same? On a modern periodic table, label the dates when 10 of the elements were discovered. How are new elements discovered and added to the periodic table? Write a report and make a poster display to illustrate your findings.

Research Ideas

2. Each element has a story to tell. Pick one element from the periodic table to research. When was it discovered? How did the element get its name? What are its properties? What are its uses? Is the element found in any common materials? How is it obtained? Report your findings in the form of a story written from the element's point of view.

3. That's a killer element! Some transition metals, including cadmium, nickel, mercury, and lead, are hazardous to human health. Find out more about how these elements are used and why they are dangerous. Write a brochure that outlines the precautions one should take to prevent poisoning people and polluting the environment when using these metals.

4. Did you know that your blood is full of metal? Your body needs iron to stay healthy. Most of the iron in the body is found in *hemoglobin*, the chemical in red blood cells that carries oxygen and carbon dioxide in your blood. Find out more about the properties of elemental iron and the compound hemoglobin. How much iron do you need daily? Where do you get iron in your diet? Write your findings in the form of a magazine article.

PHYSICAL SCIENCE

PROJECT
63 **STUDENT WORKSHEET**

The Wonders of Water

What is the difference between a pile of water molecules and a water droplet? Is there a difference? Certainly! When five or fewer water molecules group together, they bond tightly in a cluster. However, when a sixth molecule joins in, everything changes. The bonds between molecules break and re-form, causing structures that give a water droplet its round shape. It is the bonds between the water molecules as well as the bonds within a single molecule that give water its unique properties.

Ice Demystified

1. Water is odd when it comes to one particular property— freezing. The solid form of most substances is more dense than its liquid form, but not so with water! Have you ever wondered why ice floats in water? Well, between water molecules, there are weak bonds called *hydrogen bonds*. Research these bonds. How do they work? Build a model of water molecules that demonstrates hydrogen bonding, and write your findings as a newspaper article.

Another Research Idea

2. What do *fuzzyballs* and *buckyballs* have to do with chemical bonding? Each are nicknames for different forms of fullerenes. Diamonds, graphite, and fullerenes are very different substances, but they are all made of carbon atoms. Find out more about the discovery and use of fullerenes. How are the atoms in diamonds, graphite, and fullerenes arranged? How do the properties of the substances differ? Present your findings to the class in an oral presentation.

Long-Term Project Idea

3. Does your tap water conduct electricity? Find out by building your own tester! Use scissors to strip 1 cm of insulation from each end of three 10 cm lengths of copper wire. Use one wire to connect one terminal of a small flashlight bulb socket and bulb to one terminal of a dry cell. Attach the second wire to the other terminal of the socket. Attach the third wire to the vacant terminal of the dry cell. Prepare three small beakers of the following solutions: distilled water, sodium chloride, and sugar. Dip the free ends of the wires into each solution. Now use your tester to determine which solutions conduct an electric current. Collect water from a variety of sources: the tap, a pond, a lake, a spring, the ocean, or even collect some rain water. Check each sample with your tester. In which solutions does the bulb glow? Why? Present your results in a magazine article.

USEFUL TERM

fullerenes
a class of molecules; soccer-ball-shaped forms of carbon with extraordinary stability

INTERNET KEYWORDS

Buckminster Fuller

fullerenes

MATERIALS

- scissors
- metric ruler
- 30 cm insulated copper wire
- flashlight socket
- flashlight bulb
- dry cells
- 3 small beakers
- distilled water
- sugar
- sodium chloride (table salt)

PROJECT
64 **STUDENT WORKSHEET**

DESIGN
YOUR OWN

Fruitful Chemistry

Have you ever wondered why bruised apples turn brown? It's actually the result of a common type of chemical reaction. When the skin of an apple is broken, even slightly, oxygen is allowed to contact the fleshy part of the fruit. Certain chemical compounds in the fruit react with the oxygen in a process called oxidation. Once the exposed tissues are oxidized, they turn an unappetizing shade of brown. The same thing happens when you leave cut apples out for a few minutes. But never fear—lemons can save the day! Because citric acid oxidizes very quickly, lemon juice (which contains citric acid) can be used to "shield" a fruit from turning brown. This is why sliced apples coated with lemon juice last longer.

Cooking Up Chemical Reactions

1. Did you know that there's a way to cook fish without using heat? Actually, there are many interesting chemical reactions in the world of food. Research the chemistry of food and cooking. What happens when food is cooked? Why do we marinate meat in vinegar? How do you cook without applying heat? Give an in-class demonstration of cooking without heat.

Other Research Ideas

2. Fireflies need no flashlights thanks to a chemical process called *bioluminescence*. Investigate the phenomenon of bioluminescence. Why do fireflies need it? Are there any other organisms that use it? How can a chemical reaction that gives off light occur without absorbing or producing heat? Share your findings with your class by making a poster and giving an oral presentation.

Long-Term Project Idea

3. Making your own soap is an adventure! Research soap-making and soap. How did people clean things before the development of modern detergents? How does soap remove dirt? What are the essential ingredients in soap? What chemical reactions take place when soap is made? How does the addition of other ingredients improve the performance of the soap? With the help of an adult, make your own soap. You might want to use a recipe from a soap-making book or experiment to create your own recipe. Design an experiment to test the effectiveness of your homemade soap against store-bought brands. How are the soaps similar? Prepare a visual presentation to show the details of your soapy adventure with the class.

INTERNET KEYWORDS

bioluminescence
bioluminescent

SAFETY ALERT

Soap recipes usually call for lye, also known as sodium hydroxide. Lye is a strong base and can cause burns. Always wear safety goggles and protective gloves when working with lye.

PHYSICAL SCIENCE

PROJECT

65 **STUDENT WORKSHEET**

DESIGN
YOUR OWN

Tiny Plastic Factories

What do bacteria and plastic bags have in common? Well, plastics are a type of chemical compound called a *polymer*. And, certain bacteria produce polymers. Most of the plastic items we use are made out of human-made polymers that are very difficult to break down. These plastics may sit in landfills for decades and never decompose. Scientists are researching ways to use bacterial polymers to create biodegradable plastics. These plastics are more easily broken down than the plastics that crowd our landfills. Biodegradable plastics, such as those made by bacteria, may be the answer to some of our landfill problems. We know how to get the bacteria to make the polymers, but how do you think we can get the bacteria to make them in the shape of a bag?!

USEFUL TERM

biodegradable
capable of being
decomposed by
microorganisms

A Plastic World

1. Find out some other approaches to making biodegradable plastics. What makes a plastic able to break down? Does the use of biodegradable plastics solve all landfill problems associated with plastics? Could biodegradable plastics have a negative effect on the environment? Write an environmental science article explaining the kinds of biodegradable plastics that may be used in the future.

Another Research Idea

2. The Federal Mining Act of 1872 states that anyone has the right to stake a mining claim on public land if a "valuable deposit" is discovered. However, the law has no provisions for environmental protection. As a result, many mines pollute their environments with acidic wastewater runoff and cyanide. Research the debate over whether the Federal Mining Act of 1872 should be changed, and write a newspaper article that presents your findings.

Long-Term Project Idea

3. Plastics have a history! Research the history of plastics beginning with the invention of celluloid in 1869. What were the first items to be made from plastics? What were the most important breakthroughs in the development of plastic materials? How many different types of plastics exist? What advantages are there to using plastics over other materials? What are some of the byproducts of plastic manufacturing? Create a three-dimensional timeline with samples of plastics from different points in history.

PROJECT
66 **STUDENT WORKSHEET**

DESIGN YOUR OWN

Meltdown!

The worst nuclear power plant accident in the history of the United States occurred on March 28, 1979, at Three Mile Island, near Harrisburg, Pennsylvania. A series of mechanical, electrical, and human errors led to the release of radioactive gases and water into the environment. Just 7 years later, the nuclear power plant in Chernobyl, USSR, exploded, forcing almost 5 million people to evacuate the area. These accidents and other issues make the use of nuclear energy too risky to some, while others consider it one of the cleanest, safest options.

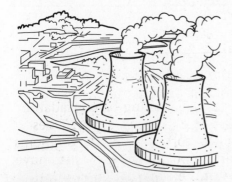

Dueling Accidents

1. Using library resources and the Internet, compare and contrast the accidents at Chernobyl and Three Mile Island. In each case, what events led to the accident? What is a core meltdown? Could the accidents have been avoided? What methods were used to clean up the sites? Are the sites still dangerous? What did nuclear scientists learn from these disasters? Present your findings in an oral presentation with visual aids.

Other Research Ideas

2. In the 1940s, a group of scientists worked together in universities and in the deserts of New Mexico on a secret war project called the Manhattan Project. Research what they were doing, who was involved, and what their goals were. Write a newspaper story as if you were a reporter writing in 1944 and you just discovered this secret project.

3. Research the work of a pioneer in the field of radioactivity. Antoine-Henri Becquerel, Marie Curie, Otto Hahn, Ernest Rutherford, Bertram Borden Boltwood, and Lise Meitner are all good subjects. Write a short biography of the scientist that you chose. Be sure to include how his or her contributions fit into the history of radioactivity research.

Long-Term Project Idea

4. Research the element radon and the problem with radon in the home. What is radon? How does it end up in our homes? Why is it dangerous to be exposed to high levels of radon? How long have we known about its dangers? Obtain a radon-detection kit, examine its contents, and read the directions. Then, test your home for radon and analyze the results. Report your findings as an article for the school newspaper.

INTERNET KEYWORDS

2. atomic energy
Chernobyl
Three Mile Island

3. Manhattan Project
J. Robert
Oppenheimer

4. radon
contamination
radon exposure

PHYSICAL SCIENCE

PROJECT
67 **STUDENT WORKSHEET**

DESIGN YOUR OWN

The Future Is Electric

If you've ever been stuck in traffic with the windows rolled down, you know how noxious the fumes from a car's exhaust can be. Not only do the fumes smell bad, but they're bad for the environment as well. And the fossil fuels that power our cars and trucks today won't be around forever. What can we do about these problems? Well, many people think that electric cars may be the answer. Several car companies and research groups have been experimenting with designs for clean, reliable electric automobiles for several years. Who knows, maybe someday you'll drive a car that you plug in instead of filling up!

Clean Driving

1. Using the library and the Internet, research electric cars. When was the first electric car built? How many different electric car designs can you find? What technological advances have made electric cars more realistic? How far and how fast can electric cars go? Are there any electric cars on the market today? How is the electricity for these cars generated? Does this cause pollution? Give an oral presentation to the class, and include visual aids.

INTERNET KEYWORD
solar salt pond

Long-Term Project Ideas

2. Electricity from a salt pond? In Israel, test sites at the Dead Sea have used a salt pond to generate small amounts of electricity. The pond acts as a solar collector. Solar ponds have been built around the world. Research how they work and what locations make a good solar pond. Build a model of a solar salt pond, and design an experiment that tests whether it is a better solar collector than a similar body of fresh water.

3. You can't always wire something the way you want. Research the local building codes for electrical wiring. Begin by calling the city or village hall and asking which department is responsible for inspecting electrical wiring. Or, interview a building inspector about the local codes for electrical wiring. Create a brochure explaining the importance of building codes to new home owners.

4. You've been told that you are not supposed to use electrical equipment near water. Do you know why? Research the safety precautions that you should take when using electrical equipment and the science behind those precautions. Create a pamphlet of safety precautions people should follow when handling electric equipment.

*DESIGN
YOUR OWN*

EMFs—Peril or Paranoia?

Are power lines deadly? Some people think so, yet others say that these fears are not supported by science. At issue are the electromagnetic fields (EMFs) generated by the electric current in high-voltage power lines.

For years some people have claimed that these magnetic fields cause cancer and other diseases in people who live near them. However, over 18 years of scientific study has led most researchers to conclude that there is no link between EMFs and cancer. Some scientists have even suggested that EMFs actually have health *benefits*! For now, at least, the search for the truth continues.

Keeping Up with Current Events

1. Even though funding for research on the EMF/cancer connection has been reduced, many people still believe that more research needs to be done on the issue. Research the ongoing debate on this topic. How have scientists studied the problem? How conclusive is their evidence? What proof do people present to support the theory that EMFs cause cancer? What do you think about the issue? Write a newspaper article to present your findings.

More Research Ideas

2. Have you ever ridden on a train? If so, you may have been impressed with how fast it went. (Or maybe you wished it could go faster!) Well, recent innovations may make it possible for trains to travel three times faster than most do today! Some American trains are expected to reach speeds of up to 500 km/h (310 mi/h)! Some of these trains will use a technology called *maglev* (magnetic levitation) to reduce friction and thus increase speed. Using the library and the Internet, research maglev trains. Find out how electromagnetic technology is helping trains go faster. Where is it being used? How long has it been around? Share your findings in the form of a magazine article.

Long-Term Project Idea

3. Did you know that you can build a motor from scratch? Research simple motors and build your own. You should be able to make a motor using little more than a D-cell battery, some wire, and a magnet. Or be creative and come up with your own materials and design! Just make sure that your motor has a part that spins when an electric current is applied. Create a poster that explains how your motor works, and share your finished motor with the class.

PHYSICAL SCIENCE

Name _____ Date _____ Class _____

DESIGN YOUR OWN

Ancient Electronics

It is A.D. 3001, and Arcturian archeologist Aldous Shuxley has just landed on planet Earth, where he plans to study ancient American culture. Shuxley finds a city that appears to have been abandoned around the year 2005.

He enters the first dwelling he sees. Inside, he discovers a device housed in a hard, plastic case. The device is small enough for a person to hold in the palm of their hand, and it has a number of buttons on its surface.

When Dr. Shuxley returns to the lab and takes the device apart, he realizes that it is an ancient piece of electronic equipment containing semiconductors. He is thrilled at such a rare find. No one has used semiconductor technology in over 500 years!

Dr. Shuxley is intrigued. What is the strange device? And how did ancient humans use it?

It's New to Me

1. Pick a common electronic device that you think Shuxley might have found, such as a cassette player, answering machine, or garage door opener. Use the Internet and library resources to find out how it works. What is the history of the device? When was it invented? Describe the device's earliest form. What effects has the device had on society? Present your findings in the form of a newspaper article.

Another Research Idea

2. Ever wonder where all the stuff that goes into electronics comes from? Pick an electronic component, such as a vacuum tube, gas tube, semiconductor, or transistor, and find out what trace materials are used to make it. You may want to contact the company that makes it. Where do the minerals come from? How difficult are they to find? Is there a reliable source for these minerals? Are any electronics in jeopardy of becoming obsolete because the trace minerals required are becoming harder to find? Make a poster showing where minerals used in electronics are found and what devices they are used in.

Long-Term Project Idea

3. Who writes computer games? Using the library or the Internet, research computer games. Arrange an interview, either in person or on-line, with a game programmer. Find out what is involved in the creation of a computer game. What kind of research is required? How many different people work on a typical game? What kinds of hardware and software are used? How long does it usually take to create a new game? Present your findings as a "how to" lesson for aspiring game producers.

PROJECT
70
STUDENT WORKSHEET

DESIGN YOUR OWN

It's a Whale of a Wave

On June 15, 1896, the fishermen working 20 km off the coast of Honshu, Japan's main island, didn't even notice the wave gently passing under their boat. However, when they returned later that day to the port city of Sanriku, they were bewildered by what they saw. The wave that passed under their boat had been a tsunami, a huge wave caused by an underwater disturbance such as an earthquake or volcano. It had grown taller as it neared the shore, killing 28,000 people and destroying 200 km of coastline.

Tsunami Trouble

1. Tsunamis travel far across the ocean without losing much energy. They can move at 700 km/h, and reach a height of 30 m on shore! Find out more about the worst tsunami disasters in history. What measures are being taken today to protect communities at risk? Write a fictional first-person account of a tsunami disaster based on your research.

Other Research Ideas

2. Did you know that waves can heal? Ultrasound technology, which uses sound waves with frequencies of 20,000 Hz and above, has a number of medical uses. For example, physicians use ultrasound waves to "shatter" kidney stones and some types of tumors without surgery. Find out more about how ultrasound works and how it is used in other medical situations. Prepare a poster to display your findings.

3. Can noise be harmful to your health? Unfortunately, yes. What health problems besides hearing loss can be caused by too much noise? Research the Noise Control Act and learn about the measures that the Environmental Protection Agency uses to control noise pollution. Present your findings in the form of a magazine article.

Long-Term Project Idea

4. What do a piano tuner, a geologist, an air traffic controller, and an EKG technician have in common? They all use their knowledge of waves to help them every day at work. Videotape an interview with a member of one of these professions. If possible, ask the person to demonstrate what he or she does at work. To prepare for your interview, research the skills involved in one of these professions and write a list of questions. Share your interview tape with your class.

INTERNET KEYWORDS

Noise Control Act
noise pollution

PHYSICAL SCIENCE

DESIGN YOUR OWN

The Caped Ace Flies Again

Narrator: Good evening, and welcome to Radio KAPE for another episode of *The Caped Ace*. [whooshing air] The Ace flies through the city, searching for those in need. No danger is too great for our valiant hero. [child crying] It isn't long before he hears the faint sounds of distress with his super-sensitive super-ears. Finally, he spots the trouble.

Ace: Never fear, I am here! [flapping cape]

Child: Aaack! Who are you, and why are you wearing pajamas?

Ace: 'Tis I, the Caped Ace, here to help you. [twinkle]

Child: I can't get my bike to work, and I'm late for school. [clank of bike]

Ace: It looks like you're missing a wheel. [metallic clanging]

Child: Yeah, that's what I thought.

Ace: Well, I always keep a spare in my superhero kit. Here. [repair noises]

Child: Wow! Thanks, Caped Ace!

SUGGESTED MATERIALS

- metal cans
- cardboard
- cord
- drinking glasses
- wooden blocks
- chopsticks
- PVC pipes
- plastic combs
- stones
- wire
- rubber bands
- wax paper

Sound Stage

1. Ever wonder how those crazy sounds on the radio are made? Research how sound effects are produced. Write a script for a 2–3 minute skit that has at least 15 homemade sound effects. Perform your drama once behind a screen that allows your classmates to hear each sound. After the performance, ask your classmates to guess how each sound was made. Then perform the skit again, this time letting them see how you created the sound effects.

Another Long-Term Project Idea

2. How can you change a sound's pitch? Create your own musical instrument. Use the suggested materials or other materials available. Be creative. Then, using an acoustic guitar tuner or a piano tuner, see how many different notes you can play. Can you play a full octave? How do you control the pitch of the sound? Create a guide to accompany your instrument.

Research Ideas

3. How does your brain know where a sound comes from? How is the pinna involved? Find out how the nerves associated with hearing are arranged and how this arrangement helps you locate sounds. Prepare an oral presentation of your findings.

4. Ever wonder how owls are able to sneak up on their prey? They are masters of soundless flight. Find out how owls fly without making a sound. Compare owl flight to the "noisy" flight of other birds, and present your findings on a poster.

The Image of the Future

Have you ever seen a hologram? Holograms are colorful 3-D pictures. You may have seen them on the covers of books and magazines; they can also be found everywhere from driver's licenses and credit cards to fighter-jet cockpits to lollipops! And the possibilities for the future use of holograms are extremely promising. In fact, if you have the time, patience, and resources, you can even make a hologram of your own!

INTERNET KEYWORDS
holography
holograms

The Light Fantastic

1. Find out more about holograms and holography. When were they invented? Why? What were the early uses of holograms? How are they created? What optical properties does holography depend on? How many different types of holograms are there? How will holograms be used in the future? Present your findings to the class in an oral presentation with visual aids.

More Research Ideas

2. Do you think only superheroes can see in the dark? Not so! Infrared technology has brought us many amazing inventions. These devices allow us not only to see in the dark but also to see many other things we wouldn't normally be able to detect. Research infrared technology in the library and/or on the Internet. Who uses these new devices? What new applications are being developed? Present your findings as a magazine article.

3. Every color of paint has a different history. Find out about the history of pigments used in painting. Where did ancient people get the pigments they used in painting? What colors were rarest during different eras, and why? What color is "mummy," and how did it come by that name? Where do modern paint pigments come from? Present your findings with a poster.

Long-Term Project Idea

4. Have you ever wanted to get a better look at your insides? Nuclear magnetic resonance spectroscopy is a powerful tool in medicine. You may have heard it called MRI—magnetic resonance imaging. Unlike X rays, which show only bone and other dense tissue, MRI allows imaging of soft tissues. Research how this process works. What kind of information can be gathered from the process? Create a list of questions for an MRI technician. Arrange a tour and an interview at a nearby hospital or clinic. Videotape your interview, and share it with your class.

PHYSICAL SCIENCE

PROJECT
73 **STUDENT WORKSHEET**

Island Vacation

For summer vacation Bogo's family has decided to stay on a deserted island. He brought some film, but forgot to pack a camera! They will be camping for several weeks on the island, and there will be no way to get a camera until he returns to the mainland. There will be very little to do besides hiking and cooking, so Bogo decides to spend his time making a pinhole camera and experimenting with it. After a few minutes of rifling through the camping supplies that his family brought, he's fairly certain that he has what he will need to make a usable camera.

SUGGESTED MATERIALS

- 1 cartridge of 110 or 126 film
- stiff corrugated cardboard
- ruler
- scissors
- electrical tape
- thumbtack or needle
- aluminum foil
- glue stick
- 2 large rubber bands
- coin
- black construction paper

Smile, You're in a Pinhole Camera!

1. Using the library or the Internet, find out how to make a pinhole camera. You will need materials similar to those shown at left. Using your research, design and build a pinhole camera. Then experiment with your camera. Try taking pictures of the same object, using different exposure times, then try widening the size of the pinhole. You should make a note of the exposure time, the size of the pinhole, the location, and the frame number for each picture you take. Remember to remove the film in a dark room. Then have your film developed. Make a display that includes a description of how a pinhole camera works and the pictures that you took.

Research Ideas

2. What happens to your film after you drop it off to be developed? Find out! How does photographic film capture an image? How does the size of the film affect the picture quality? How do black-and-white film and color film differ in how they are made, how they capture images, and how they are developed? Present your findings to the class with plenty of examples.

3. What are the facts on faxing? You can place a document in a machine and only seconds later a copy, or facsimile (fax), comes out on a machine hundreds of kilometers away. How is that possible? Research how facsimile machines work. Build a model or draw a diagram to illustrate what you have learned.

4. Lasers are used for a variety of medical procedures including vision correction, early detection of lung cancer tumors, and improvement of tooth surfaces—to name just a few! Research how lasers are used in medicine. Why are different kinds of lasers needed for different procedures? Create a poster display to illustrate your findings.